The New York Times

Country Music's Greatest Songs

93 songs arranged for piano, voice and guitar

Edited by Milton Okun

Times BOOKS

Acknowledgments:

Once again I must thank a most valuable and competent team of associates for their assistance and resourcefulness: Jean Dinegar, Dan Fox, Lauren Keiser, Pat Raven and Mary Ann Tiernan-O'Grady. As to Messrs. Tom Lipscomb, Len Schwartz and Murray Frank, their encouragement and prodding really paid off with not one but two books of the greatest songs—Country Music's and those very special remembrances of the Seventies!

Also, my appreciation to those publishers who have cooperated so generously in making this collection possible.
Milton Okun

Library of Congress Catalog Card Number: 78-58169.

ISBN: 0-8129-6312-1

Manufactured in the United States of America.

Photographs courtesy of *The New York Times*.

Contents

Introduction

To take the long view, *The New York Times Country Music's Greatest Songs* is the result of three great historic events and a whole lot of harmless musical fooling around during idle times.

The first great historic event took place in the Eighteenth Century when the British Government attempted to disperse the Scottish Tribes after the Jacobean uprisings of 1715 (The Old Pretender) and 1745 (Bonnie Prince Charlie). Many Scots, discouraged by the English attempts to stop border raids and border contraband, had already moved to Ireland. Here they found the colleens congenial, but the English laws still intolerable. In the latter part of the century there was a great movement of Scots and Irish, and Scots-Irish to the New World where they found the New England Anglicans not only in possession of all the good land but as unreceptive to their Calvinist ways as had been the British themselves.

And so they pushed on, these Scots-Irish, taking with them what little they had: a proud heritage of independence, a few iron pots, a spotted hog, and their music. Sometimes they managed to bring a musical instrument too, but these were hard times, naked times, and if the choice came between a kid or a piglet or a bagpipe, the bagpipe was left behind.

Through the Cumberland Gap they came and spread out through the hill country of Kentucky and Tennessee, of North and South Carolina. Tragically unaware of the richness of this new world, they frequently chose the wrong site for the family farm, ignoring the rich bottom lands in favor of the thin-soiled highlands (The Ridge Runners), or settling in barren hollows that reminded them of the Scottish Highlands. Here they settled in proud isolation in a land that was already oriented toward the West, toward the abundances of gold and the fertility of the Middle Border.

Their Fundamentalist beliefs supported them in their poverty and isolation *(Amazing Grace)*, but these same beliefs also contributed to their troubles: too many children on a small farm, for example. The drain of manpower to the city began early. The father might in despair take to drink *(Please Daddy, Don't Get Drunk This Christmas)*, or simply desert to the jobs in the city. If the father didn't go then the older sons did...and all of this is recorded in their music. It is a music filled with longing, nostalgia, sorrow and lamentation for a lost Eden of childhood *(Take Me Home, Country Roads)*. But never despair! There is not only the sound of saving grace in their music, there is endemic to it a unique country humor.

The Country Rube is hanging on the split-rail fence
when the City Feller sluffs up.
"Hey, how long until I get to the next town?"
But the Rube doesn't answer, just stands there with
his wrists dangling down.
"To hell," says the City Feller and starts off. At
the edge of the property, the Rube calls him back.
"An hour and a half to the next town," he says.
"Why didn't you tell me that before?"
"I didn't know how fast you could walk."

There it is, caught in a joke, the pride, the independence, the isolation, the humor, and the Fundamentalist belief in *truth*.

During this time of isolation the country folk developed their own music and new musical instruments. Music was required for hoedowns and harvest festivals and marriage celebrations; but there were the everyday occupations that required song, too: cradle rocking, butter churning, plowing and game playing. Because of the isolation of the people who created them, the country songs retained an Elizabethan flavor, although they were adapted to new musical instruments: the five-string banjo, the harmonica and the dulcimer.

World War II was the second great historical event that changed the course of country music. That war changed the face of the Western Hemisphere, so, of course, it made its impact on country music, too. One can say with some precision what World War II did for country music: It wasn't a change in music or theme or instrumentation; World War II gave country music a national audience.

Before the war, when rural boys had migrated to the cities they had been in search of jobs and they had either hunkered down in some comfortably rural suburb, or they had divested themselves of rural ways, rural music and overalls, to compete for the jobs available to them *(Detroit City)*. The young men who were drafted in wartime saw no reason to camouflage their origin. They were in for the duration; they would fight as their daddies had done in the Great War (Sergeant Alvin York was honored at the premiere of the 1940 movie *The Grand Ole Opry)*, and then they would return to their hollers and farms. There was no need to seek camouflage; they brought with them into the army their music, their instruments, their Fundamentalist beliefs and their humor.

At induction centers and training camps, the hillbilly suddenly emerged. At one induction camp a country boy sat at the head of the line. He sat on the floor, his legs stretched out in front of him in a country manner, and he thoughtfully fingered the day's growth of his beard. "I thought to shave before I came," he announced loudly, "but then I thought to wait till after I was inducted and so do it on company time." The hillbilly had come out of the holler.

Country music was heard in army camps all over America, on North Atlantic transports, in staging camps in England and, finally, on the European Continent itself. American Forces Air Stations played *The Wabash Cannonball.*

There was a reverse movement, too. Hundreds of thousands of urban boys found themselves encamped at southern army bases. At Fort Bragg and Fort Benning, where the local radios played country music, the soldier boys from the Bronx and Berkeley might find themselves humming *Roving Gambler* as they shaved. And after the war, not all the country boys returned to their hollers. As a guess, something like ninety-nine percent of the country boys stationed at Lowery Field outside of Denver, Colorado, returned to Denver to live after the war: blue skies, federal jobs, and a Rocky Mountain high.

Henry J. Deutschendorf, Jr., chose his singing name wisely: John Denver. He is in the mainstream of the new country music that is the result of the third historic event: the introduction of the transistor radio.

Isolation was swept away by the transistor radio. Whereas the wartime dislocation of the population brought country music to the city, the transistor radio brought city music to the hollers. The country boys who had heard only the music of their daddies and of the courtesy uncles (Uncle Dave Macon, for instance) suddenly heard in the hollers Honky-Tonk, Rock and Roll, and the strange folk music of Harry Belafonte singing the Jamaican *Come, Tally Me Bananas.* Country music has never been the same.

But the strength of the traditional country music is shown in this collection; country music has *absorbed* innovations—Swing, Honky-Tonk, Western and Rock and Roll rhythms, and electronic amplification—and yet country music has remained true to the spirit of its origins. The songs in this collection are not very much like the songs that Alan Lomax collected when he first penetrated the Appalachians looking for *folk* music, but these songs are legitimate heirs of that music.

That music was caught and preserved for us all as some kind of a national monument by Alan Lomax, who, as a graduate student at Harvard under the tutelage of George Lyman Kitteridge, came first to wonder at what Bishop Percy had done in the Eighteenth Century in collecting the Border Ballads of Scotland and England. Together, graduate student and professor came to the realization that there was the opportunity in the isolated Appalachians to reproduce Bishop Percy's experience in collecting traditional songs. But they had a new and thrilling instrument: the Edison Recording Machine. Alan Lomax, a recording machine strapped on his back, heavy wet-cell batteries carried in either hand, slogged through the hollers and climbed the ridges, recording songs that were still truly Elizabethan and still sung in the Seventeenth Century manner, the body tightly held, the voices tight and pitched so high that some men sang a falsetto. The style has changed, but the songs are true to the source in their melodic ornamentation and in their themes. Like so many of the songs of a simple people, *Ode to Billy Joe* speaks of death and separation and unrequited love, just as did *Bonny Barbara Allen,* collected by Bishop Percy in the Eighteenth Century and again by Alan Lomax in the Twentieth.

> O mother, mother make my bed!
> O make it soft and narrow!
> My love has died for me today,
> I'll die for him tomorrow.

Unrequited love is the theme of *Another Somebody Done Somebody Wrong Song, Linda on My Mind* and *Today I Started Loving You Again.* Sometimes the longing of such love turns to sentimentality, but sometimes it turns to violence, too, and that brings us to another common theme of country music: the wandering outlaw. In the Seventeenth Century it was Robin Hood:

> Come, listen to me, you gallants so free,
> All you that loves mirth for to hear,
> And I will tell you of a bold outlaw,
> That lived in Nottinghamshire.

In the Twentieth Century it could be the violent lover, the roving gambler, the anti-establishment outlaw (Dillinger, Bonnie and Clyde), or the rootless hobo driven by poverty as in the *The Wabash Cannonball.*

> Listen to the jingle, the rumble and the roar,
> Riding through the woodlands to the hills and by the shore.
> Hear the mighty rush of the engine, hear the lonesome hobo squall,
> Riding through the jungle on the Wabash Cannonball.

But the establishment is, after all, in charge of things and doesn't, by and large, approve of the romantic outlaw, so the next great theme in country music is the prison song—a natural consequence of the previous theme. *Folsom Prison Blues* is one such song; other songs not in this collection are *Columbus Jailhouse* and *Midnight Special.* Johnny Cash's famous recording of *A Boy Named Sue* was made in Folsom Prison before an audience of prisoners, and the real electricity, the excitement of that recording, lies in the audience's wildly approving response. Whoops of pleasure and thunderous applause mark the audience's recognition of itself in the "scalawag father," in the "avenging son" and in the "barroom battlers" fighting in "the mud and the blood and the beer." Near the end of the recording, Johnny Cash identifies himself with the prisoners by stepping out of line, by deliberately breaking a broadcasting taboo, to sing of "the (bleep) that named me Sue." The laughter is generous, but the climax of the audience reaction comes at the very end of the song where hard-earned common sense and folk wisdom wins out over tricky rationalization. "If I have a son, I'm gonna name him…Bill or George, or anything but Sue."

Love of the land is one of the most enduring of the country music themes; sometimes it is combined with a nostalgia for the simple ways of remembered childhood *(Oklahoma Hills),* but sometimes there is a wry, humorous note that acknowledges the hardships of country living, and still plumps for that life as the best, *Thank God I'm A Country Boy* and *Everything Is Beautiful.* Sometimes the love of the land gets mixed up with the country ways of Fundamentalist religion and conservative politics and then there emerges the proud, flaunting satire of an *Okie from Muskogee.*

Of course, there have been changes in the music and in the themes. Some of the changes are obvious: The railroad has disappeared as a romantic image, and Casey Jones and the hobo have given way to the trucker and the hitch-hiker. The place of women has altered, too, in country music. A generation ago, woman was still the support of man, helpmate and quiet encourager:

"That's okay," Rose would say,
"Don't you worry none.
We'll have good time by and by
When the work is done."

In recent country songs the voice of woman has sounded clearly for herself. There is little subtlety to Loretta Lynn's *Don't Come Home A-Drinkin' (With A-Lovin' on Your Mind)*. Her song *The Pill* makes a little broader statement about women's place.

But even the songs that might be seen as songs of Women's Liberation fit into the old thematic patterns. *Harper Valley PTA* is couched in modern terms but it is a marvelous example of reversed terminology. The mother, beset by the hard-nosed PTA, is in fact a female Robin Hood, a romantic outlaw, who, in a wondrous reversal, is attacking the spiritually impoverished to give spiritual riches to her child. In country music, as in everything else, everything changes but change.

It used to be said that the aristocracy and the folk shared this one thing in common: You couldn't join them; you had to be born to them. Loretta Lynn makes this point in the title of her autobiography, *Coal Miner's Daughter;* and Burke's *Peerage* remains unshaken in its belief that birth makes the difference, not talent nor wealth. But in country music there has been a change of late: Some of the leading composers and singers have not been born to the folk. Johnny Cash, Loretta Lynn, Dolly Parton and Tom T. Hall were all, as it were, to the holler born. But there are other leading composers and singers who were not born-folk: John Denver, Shel Silverstein and Kris Kristofferson, for instance.

Before World War II, the chief musical instrument of the American home was the piano. The piano dominated the living room unless the house had been specifically designed with a "music room" that would shelter the piano. Children were taught music on the piano and at Christmas and Thanksgiving relatives sat in respectful awe as the child played his greatest triumph, *Barcarolle* from Offenbach's *Tales of Hoffmann.*

The piano was the musical instrument most commonly used to accompany singers, and at parties and reunions people gathered around the piano to sing. But all this has changed sharply since country music came out of the hills. The guitar is now the instrument that most children first learn to play and it is the guitar that is the most common musical instrument played to accompany group singing.

Country music isn't the only reason for this change. American society is much more loosely constructed and mobile now: One can sling a guitar on one's back or pitch it into the back of an RV, and the television set in the living room effectively silences the piano for many hours of the day and night. But in fraternity houses, at political rallies, and in back bedrooms where adolescents cope with the problems of growing up, it is the guitar that is heard, and, often, the sounds of country music.

Thanks to those last two great historic events described earlier in this introduction one need not be born into poverty and isolation to grow up in the country tradition. The national audience and the transistor radio make it possible for a child in Minneapolis or Denver, or even New York, to grow up with those country principles of proud independence and respect for the everyday problems of the simple folk: death, poverty, separation, and unrequited love...and to see all of them countered with humor and song.

Perhaps this book, *Country Music's Greatest Songs*, represents a fourth great historic event. We are all no longer audience to country music; we can be a part of it, contributors to that great tradition. It isn't so much that country has become national; we have been able to understand and at last enjoy and contribute to one of our oldest musical heritages. *Thank God I'm A Country Boy!*

Milton Okun

1

2

3

4

1 *The Statler Brothers*
2 *Elvis Presley*
3 *John Denver*
4 *Kenny Rogers*

1

3

4

x

5

6

7

8

9

(Hey, Won't You Play)
Another Somebody
Done Somebody Wrong Song

Words and Music by Larry Butler and Chips Moman

1

D. S. al Fine

sad — that it makes ev - 'ry - bod — y cry.____

A real hurt - in' song ____ a - bout a

love that's gone__ wrong, 'Cause I don't__ wan - na

cry all a - lone.

3

Act Naturally

Words and Music by Johnny Russell and Vonie Morrison

And all I got-ta do is act nat-'ral-
'Cause all I have to do is act nat-'ral-

1. ly. We'll
2. ly. Well, I

bet you I'm gon-na be a big star,—— Might

win an Os-car you can't nev-er tell.—— The

Before The Next Teardrop Falls

Moderately slow

Words and Music by Ben Peters and Vivian Keith

tear-drops ev – er start,⎫ I'll be there be-fore the next tear-drop
made you shed a tear,⎭

1. falls. Tho' it falls. **2.** I'll be

there an – y time you need me by your side To

dry a – way ev – 'ry tear-drop that you cried. If he

Back Home Again

Words and Music by John Denver

mile or more a - way, ___ The whin-in' of ___ his wheels ___

___ just makes it cold - er. ___ He's an

hour a - way from rid - in' ___ on your prayers up in the
all the news to tell him: ___ just spend - in' time with
sweet - est thing I know of, ___

sky; And ten days on ___ the road ___ are bare - ly
time? And what's the lat - est thing ___ the neigh-bors
you, It's the lit - tle things ___ that make ___ a house a

Battle Of New Orleans

Words and Music by Jimmy Driftwood

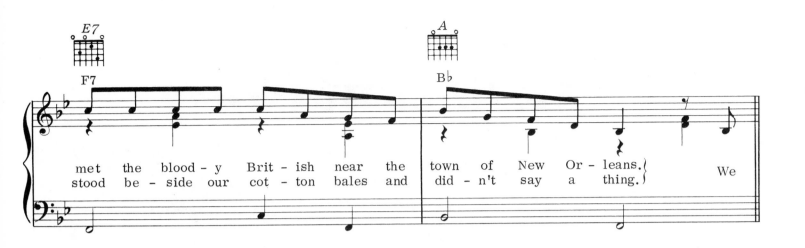

met the blood-y Brit-ish near the town of New Or-leans.}
stood be-side our cot-ton bales and did-n't say a thing.}
We

Chorus

fired our guns and the Brit-ish kept a-com-in', There wuz-n't nigh as man-y as they

wuz a while a-go. We fired once more and they be-gan to run-nin', On

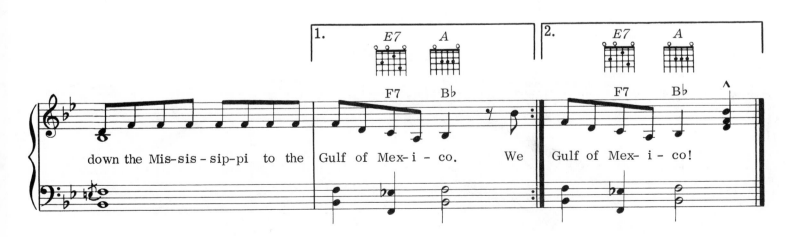

1.
down the Mis-sis-sip-pi to the Gulf of Mex-i-co. We
2.
Gulf of Mex-i-co!

Berkeley Woman

Slow Country feeling

Words and Music by Bryan Bowers

3. I fin'lly realized there was hunger in my stare,
   And in my mind I was swayin' with the woman in the rockin' chair.
   But the lady I was livin' with was standin' right by my side,
   She saw me stare and she saw my hunger, and Lord, it made her cry.

4. So with anger in her face and hurt in her eyes,
   She scratched me and she clawed me, she screamed and she cried,
   "Oh, you don't give me near all the lovin' that you should,
   Yet you're ready to go and lay with her; you're just no damn good."

5. Well, I guess she's prob'ly right, I guess I'm prob'ly wrong,
   I guess she's not too far away, she hasn't been gone very long.
   And I guess we could get together and try just one more time,
   But I know that wanderlust would come again, she'd only wind up cry'n'.

6. Now you've heard this story, plain as the light of day,
   It's hard to feel guilty for lovin' the ladies, that's all I gotta say.
   'Cept a woman is the sweetest fruit that God ever put on the vine,
   And I'd no more love just one kind-a woman than drink only one kind-a (wine.)

Daddy Sang Bass

Words and Music by Carl Perkins

geth-er in a fam - 'ly cir - cle sing - in' loud._____
geth-er a - gain up yonder in a lit - tle while._____

Chorus
Dad-dy sang bass, ma-ma sang ten-or, me and lit-tle bro-ther would join right in there;

Sing-in' seems to help a trou-bled soul._____ One of these days and it won't be

long, I'll re-join them in a song; I'm gon-na join the fam-'ly cir-cle at the

21

A Boy Named Sue

Words and Music by Shel Silverstein

23

ever did was be - fore he left, he went and named me Sue.

Verse II

2. Well, he must have thought it was quite a joke, And it

got lots of laughs from - a lots of folks, It seems I had to fight my whole life

through. Some gal would giggle and I'd get red, And

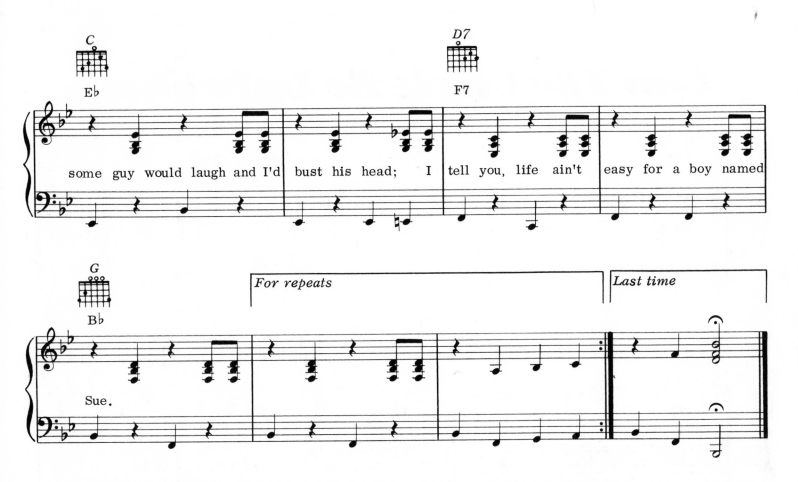

some guy would laugh and I'd bust his head; I tell you, life ain't easy for a boy named

Sue.

For repeats

Last time

3. (Well,) I grew up quick and I grew up mean, My fist got hard and my wits got keen,
Roamed from town to town to hide my shame. But I made me a vow to the moon and stars:
I'd search the honky tonks and bars and kill that man that give me that awful name.

4. But it was Gatlinburg in mid-July and I had just hit town and my throat was dry,
I'd thought I'd stop and have myself a brew. At an old saloon on a street of mud
And at a table dealing stud sat the dirty, mangy dog that named me Sue.

5. Well, I knew that snake was my own sweet dad from a worn-out picture that my mother had,
And I knew that scar on his cheek and his evil eye. He was big and bent and gray and old,
And I looked at him and my blood ran cold, and I said "My name is Sue. How do you do.
Now you're gonna die." Yeah, that's what I told him.

6. Well, I hit him right between the eyes and he went down, but to my surprise he come up with a knife
And cut off a piece of my ear. But I busted a chair right across his teeth, And we crashed through
the wall and into the street, Kicking and a-gouging in the mud and the blood and the beer.

7. I tell you I've fought tougher men but I really can't remember when,
He kicked like a mule and he bit like a crocodile. I heard him laughin' and then I heard him cussin',
He went for his gun and I pulled mine first. He stood there looking at me and I saw him smile.

8. And he said, "Son, this world is rough and if a man's gonna make it, he's gotta be tough;
And I knew I wouldn't be there to help you along. So I give you that name and I said 'Goodbye;'
I knew you'd have to get tough or die. And it's that name that helped to make you strong."

9. "Yeah," he said, "Now you have just fought one helluva fight, and I know you hate me and you've
got the right to kill me now, and I wouldn't blame you if you do. But you ought to thank me
before I die for the gravel in your guts and the spit in your eye because I'm the _ _ _ _
that named you Sue."

Yeah, what could I do? What could I do?

10. I got all choked up and I threw down my gun. Called him a pa and he called me a son,
And I come away with a different point of view. And I think about him now and then.
Every time I tried, every time I win and if I ever have a son I think I am gonna name him
Bill or George — anything but Sue.

Can The Circle Be Unbroken

Adapted and Arranged by Dan Fox

Chug-A-Lug

Words and Music by Roger Miller

Moderately, with a beat

Chorus

Crazy

Moderately slow

Words and Music by Willie Nelson

Crying Time

Words and Music by Buck Owens

Slowly, but with a lilt

Guitar → (Capo up 3 frets)

Piano →

Oh, it's cry-ing time a-gain___ you're gon-na leave me, I can
(Oh, they) say that ab-sence makes___ the heart grow fond-er, And that

see that far a-way look in your eyes. I can tell___ by the way you hold me,
tears are on-ly rain to make love grow. Well, my love for you could nev-er grow no

dar-ling,___ That it won't be long be-fore it's cry-ing
strong-er,___ If I live to be a hun-dred years___

Dang Me

Words and Music by Roger Miller

wom - an sit - tin' home____ with a month old____ child.____
lack____ four - teen dol - lars hav - in' twen - ty sev - en cents.
pap - py was a pis - tol, I'm a son - of - a - gun.____

Chorus

Dang me, dang me, they ought-ta take a rope and hang me

high from the high - est tree, Wom - an, would you weep for me!

After repeats
D. S. al Coda 𝄋

Coda

Detroit City

Words and Music by Danny Dill and Mel Tillis

Moderately

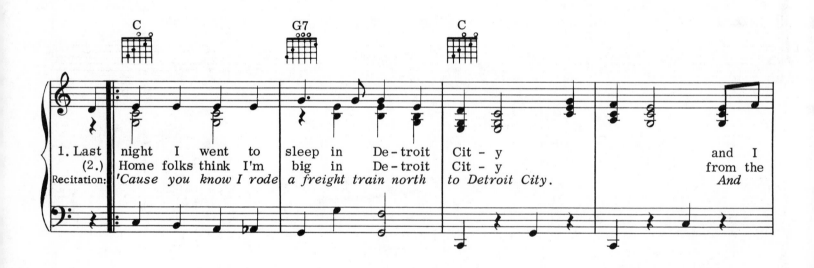

1. Last night I went to sleep in De-troit Cit - y and I
(2.) Home folks think I'm big in De-troit Cit - y from the
Recitation: *'Cause you know I rode a freight train north to Detroit City.* *And*

dreamed a - bout the cot - ton fields and home;
let - ters that I write they think I'm fine.
after all these years I *find I've just been* *wasting my time,*

I
But by
So I

dreamed a-bout my moth-er, dear old pa-pa, sis-ter and broth-er and I
day I make the cars,___ by___ night I make___ the bars;___ if
just think I'll take my foolish pride and put it on the south-bound freight and ride And

dreamed a-bout the girl who's been wait-ing for so long.) I wan-na go
on-ly they could read be-tween the___ lines.___
go on back to the loved ones, the ones that I left waiting so far behind.___

home,___ I wan-na go home;___ Oh, how I

wan - na go home.___ (2.)___ home.___

Don't It Make My Brown Eyes Blue

Words and Music by Richard Leigh

I did-n't mean to treat you bad, _____ did-n't know just

what I had, ____ But, hon-ey, now I do ____ and

don't it make my brown eyes, don't it make my brown eyes,

don't it make my brown eyes blue. And

Repeat and fade

Do You Know
You Are My Sunshine

In a bright country 2 (♩ = 1 beat)

Words and Music by Don Reid and Harold Reid

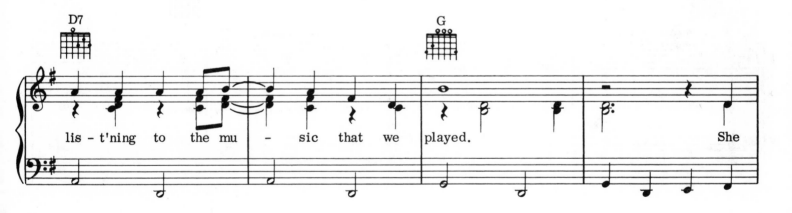

Chorus

42

would you do___ it one more time for me?"___

Bor - der to bor - der and o - cean to o - cean, I
gone just as quick___ as the song that she asked___ for,___

still look for her ev - 'ry place.___
Tak - ing my sun - shine a - way.___ But

Chas - ing the sun - shine___ each and ev - 'ry night,___ I'm
some - day when I fin - 'lly look___ down___ and see___ her,___ I

Dreams Of The Everyday Housewife

Words and Music by Chris Gantry

Bright Waltz tempo

mf

Verse *mp*

She looks in the mir - ror, and stares at the wrin - kles that
(The) pho - to - graph al - bum she takes from the clos - et, and

were - n't there yes - ter - day,_____ and thinks of the
slow - ly turns the first page;_____ And care - ful - ly

young man that she al - most mar - ried; ___ What would he think if he
picks up the crum - bl - ing flow - er; The first one he gave her, now

Easy Loving

Words and Music by Freddie Hart

ev - 'ry day's__ Thanks - giv - ing,_____ To count all the

bless - ings I would - n't know__ where to start. Ev - 'ry

time_____ I look you o - ver,_____ So real to life it

seems, Up - on your__ pret - ty shoul - ders_____ There's a

England Swings

Words and Music by Roger Miller

fin-'lly save e-nough mon-ey | up to take your fam - i - ly | on a trip a-cross the sea,___
pa-pa's mus - tache,_____ | Fall-in' out the win-dow sill, | fro-lic in the grass,_____

_____ Take a tip be-fore you | take your trip, let me tell you | where to go, Go to
Tryin' to mock the way they talk___ | but with all in vain,_____ |

En - ge-land.___ Oh, | Gap-in' at the dap-per men with | der-by hats and canes.

Coda

Whistle (8va higher on each repeat)_____
mp - p

D. S. al Coda

Repeat and fade

Every Time Two Fools Collide

Words and Music by Jeff Tweel and Jan Dyer

*Guitarists tune 6th string to D.

time! _____ I've felt_ there must be a way

that we_ still have-n't tried_____ To keep our hearts from break-in'____ ev-'ry

time two fools col - lide, To keep our hearts from break-in'_____ ev-'ry

time two fools col - lide._____

slower

Everything Is Beautiful

Words and Music by Ray Stevens

58

59

Flyin' Home To Nashville

Words and Music by Bill and Taffy Danoff

au - to - mo - tive hall of fame all framed in or - ange and
names on paint - ed bill - boards like all the cred - its flash - in' by
best of all is make - be - lieve and the worst of dreams come true

grey And the cam - 'ra slow - ly pans a - cross the
Slip - pin' in and out of fo - cus like the
So I'll say so long to Hol - ly - wood And the

air - port in L.
smog in both my
rest is up to

A.
eyes.
you.

We're all

Chorus

sing - ers in a choir, we're all play - ers in a play,

mf

The Fiddlers Of Ophir Creek

Moderately

Words and Music by Pat and Victoria Garvey

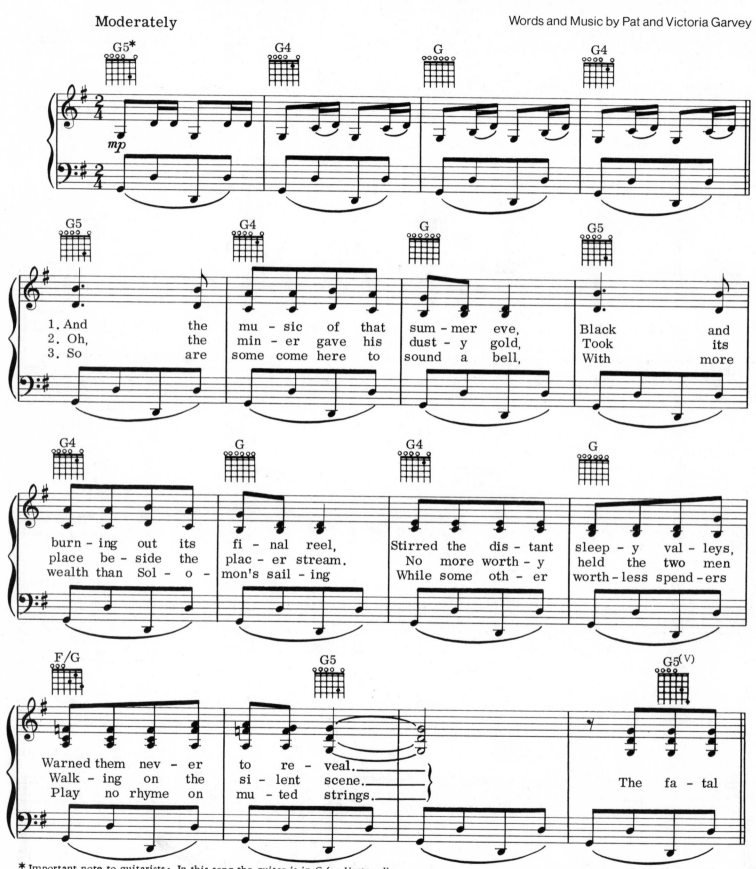

1. And the mu-sic of that sum-mer eve, Black and
2. Oh, the min-er gave his dust-y gold, Took its
3. So are some come here to sound a bell, With more

burn-ing out its fi-nal reel, Stirred the dis-tant sleep-y val-leys,
place be-side the plac-er stream. No more worth-y held the two men
wealth than Sol-o-mon's sail-ing While some oth-er worth-less spend-ers

Warned them nev-er to re-veal.
Walk-ing on the si-lent scene.
Play no rhyme on mu-ted strings.

The fa-tal

* Important note to guitarists: In this song the guitar is in G (or Vestapol)
  tuning: 6th string = D, 5th = G, 4th, 3rd, and 2nd strings unchanged.
  1st string = D. The chord diagrams are for guitar in this tuning.

Flowers On The Wall

Words and Music by Lew DeWitt

Moderately, in 2 (♩ = 1 beat)

Note: This song was recorded ½ step higher in B major. Pianists who wish to play with the record may mentally change the key signature to 5 sharps. Guitarists can capo up 4 instead of 3 frets.

flow - ers on the wall that don't both - er me at all,

Play - in' sol - i - taire till dawn with a deck of fif - ty one,

Smok - in' cig - a - rettes and watch - in' Cap - tain

Folsom Prison Blues

Words and Music by Johnny Cash

Moderately (not too slow)

Chorus

1. I hear the train a - com - in'; it's roll - in' 'round the bend, And
(2. When) I was just a ba - by my ma - ma told me, "Son, _____ And

I ain't seen the sun - shine since I don't know when. I'm
al - ways be a good boy; don't ever play with guns. But I

stuck at Fol - som Pris - on and time keeps drag - gin'
shot a man in Re - no just _____ to watch him

on. _____ But that
die. _____ When I

train ___ keeps ___ roll - in' blow - in'   on   down   to
hear that whis - tle   I   hang   my

San ___ An - tone. _____ 2. When ___
head ___ and ___ cry. _____

3. I bet there's rich folks eatin' in a fancy dining car.

  They're prob'ly drinkin' coffee and smokin' big cigars,

  But I know I had it comin', I know I can't be free,

  But those people keep a-movin', and that's what tortures me.

4. Well, if they freed me from this prison, if that railroad train was mine,

  I bet I'd move on over a little farther down the line,

  Far from Folsom Prison, that's where I want to stay,

  And I'd let that lonesome whistle blow my blues away.

Funny How Time Slips Away

Words and Music by Willie Nelson

Moderately slow

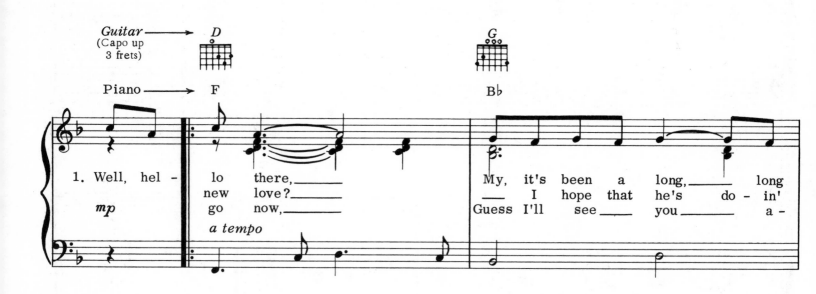

1. Well, hel- lo there,_____
   new love?_____
   go now,_____

My, it's been a long,_____ long
___ I hope that he's do- in'
Guess I'll see___ you_____ a-

time._____
fine._____
round._____

"How'm I do- in'?"_____
Heard you told him_____ that you'd
Don't know when tho'_____ Nev- er

Oh, I guess that I'm doin' fine._____ It's been so
love him till the end____ of time._____ Now that's the
know when I'll be back____ in town._____ — But re-

long now,_____ and it seems that it was on - ly yes-ter-
same thing_____ that you told me, seems like just_____ the oth - er
mem - ber _____ what I tell you, that in time_____ you're gon - na

day._____ Gee, ain't it fun - ny _____ how time slips a-
day._____ Gee, ain't it fun - ny _____ how time slips a-
pay._____ And it's sur- pris - ing_____ how time slips a-

1.2. way._____ 2. How's your way._____
way._____ 3. Got - ta

Gentle On My Mind

Words and Music by John Hartford

couch. And it's know-ing I'm not shack-led by for- got- ten words and bonds__ And the ink stains that have dried up - on some line, That__

2. It's not clinging to the rocks and ivy planted on their columns now that binds me
Or something that somebody said because they thought we fit together walkin'.
It's just knowing that the world will not be cursing or forgiving when I walk along
Some railroad track and find
That you're moving on the backroads by the rivers of my memory and for hours
You're just gentle on my mind.

3. Though the wheat fields and the clothes lines and junkyards and the highways
Come between us
And some other woman crying to her mother 'cause she turned and I was gone.
I still run in silence, tears of joy might stain my face and summer sun might
Burn me 'til I'm blind
But not to where I cannot see you walkin' on the backroads by the rivers flowing
Gentle on my mind.

4. I dip my cup of soup back from the gurglin' cracklin' caldron in some train yard
My beard a rough'ning coal pile and a dirty hat pulled low across my face.
Through cupped hands 'round a tin can I pretend I hold you to my breast and find
That you're waving from the backroads by the rivers of my memory ever smilin'
Ever gentle on my mind.

Give Me Back My Cool, Clean Water

Words and Music by Rick Shaw and Dick Clark

Moderately, in 2 (♩ = 1 beat)

mp smoothly

1. Smoke stacks belch - ing clouds of thick black smoke in - to the sky,

Cit - ies pump - ing filth in - to the riv - ers run - ning by,

High - ways lined with lit - ter, rust - y beer cans ev - 'ry - where,

*Guitarists: tune 6th string to D.

Goodbye, My Sweet Johnny

Words and Music by Jim Friedman and Tennise Broeck

Moderately, in 2 (♩ = 1 beat)

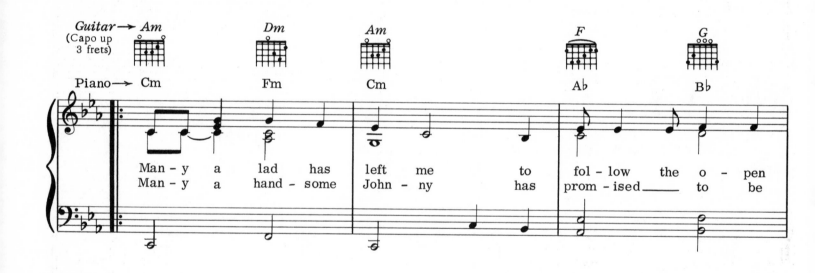

Man-y a lad has left me to fol-low the o-pen
Man-y a hand-some John-ny has prom-ised____ to be

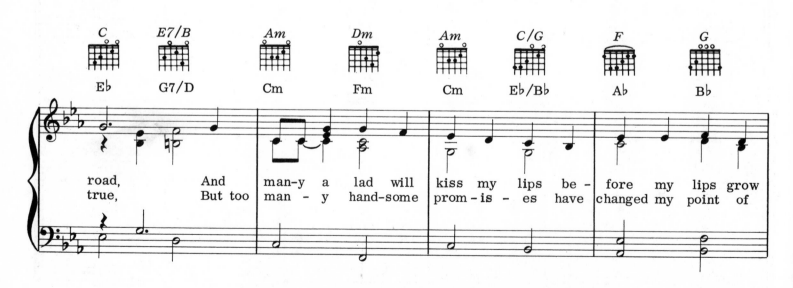

road, And man-y a lad will kiss my lips be-fore my lips grow
true, But too man-y hand-some prom-is-es have changed my point of

cold,
view. For

Many a love has touched my heart but
though any ugly duckling may_____

each was a rolling stone, And many's the lad who's
some-day___ be a swan, And though hand-some is as

sworn___ to stay And left me all a-lone. So good-
hand-some does, A John me is just a John. So heigh-

bye, my sweet Johnny, come back to me some spring, Come
ho, my sweet Johnny, heigh-ho and fare-thee-well, For

back be - fore my heart -ache is fast re - mem - ber - ing. Come
I knew all a - bout you long be - fore you rang my bell. When-

back when the wind is blow - ing the salt spray from the
ev - er the spir - it moves you, the you know I'll set you

sea, And when your wan - der - lust is gone, Sweet
free, But when you come__ a - gain, sweet John, I

1.
John come back to me.

2.
may have com - pa - ny.
slower

Gotta Travel On

Words and Music by Paul Clayton

played a-round this old town too long And I

C **D7** *To Coda* ⊕ **G**
(last time)
feel like I've got-ta tra-vel on. _____

Verse **G**

1. Pop-pa writes to John-ny, but John-ny can't come
2. High sher-iff and po-lice rid-ing af-ter
3. Want to see my hon-ey, want to see her

home. John-ny can't come home, no,
me, Rid-ing af-ter me, yes,
bad, Want to see her bad, oh,

G7

Gospel Changes

Words and Music by Jack Williams

* Guitarists: Tune lowest string to D.

Grandma's Feather Bed

Words and Music by Jim Connor

89

D.S. al Coda 𝄋

Coda 𝄌

Heartaches By The Number

Words and Music by Harlan Howard

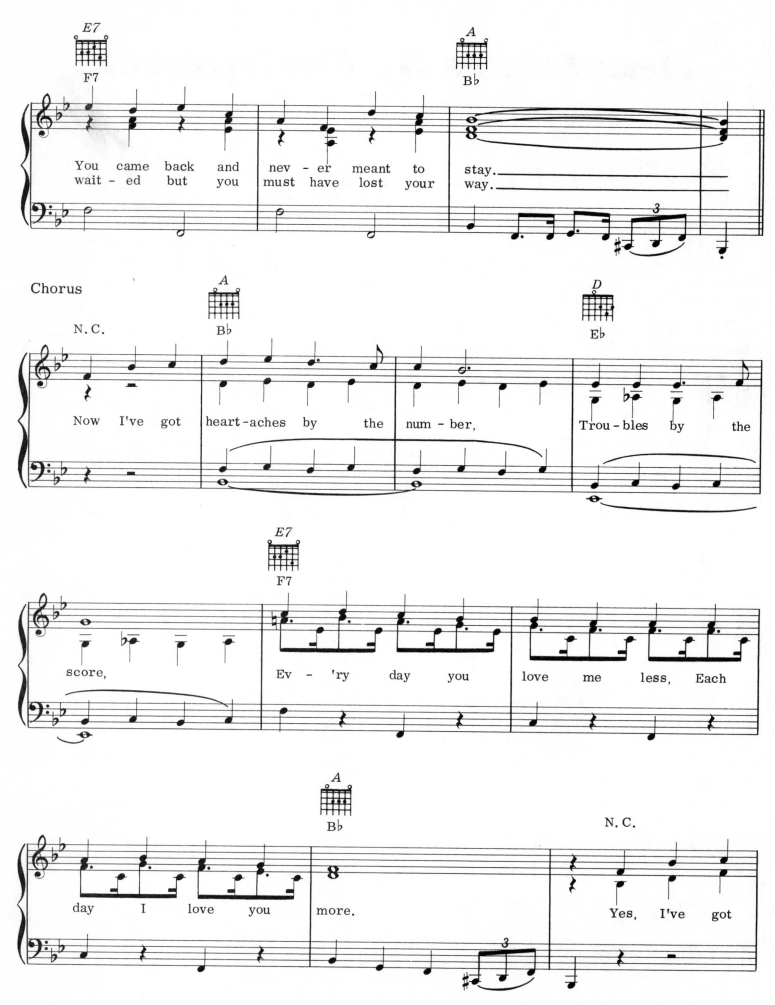

Chorus

You came back and nev-er meant to stay.
wait-ed but you must have lost to your way.

Now I've got heart-aches by the num-ber, Trou-bles by the score, Ev-'ry day you love me less, Each day I love you more.

Yes, I've got

Green, Green Grass Of Home

Words and Music by Curly Putman

Harper Valley PTA

Words and Music by Tom T. Hall

(Recitation): 2. The note said, Mrs. Johnson, you're wearing your dresses way too high—
   It's reported you've been drinking and a-runnin' 'round with men and going wild.
   We don't believe you ought to be a-bringing up your little girl this way—
   It was signed by the secretary, Harper Valley P-T.A.

3. Well, it happened that the P-T.A. was gonna meet that very afternoon—
   They were sure surprised when Mrs. Johnson wore her mini-skirt into the room.
   As she walked up to the blackboard, I still recall the words she had to say.
   She said, "I'd like to address this meeting of the Harper Valley P-T.A.

4. Well, there's Bobby Taylor sittin' there and seven times he's asked me for a date.
   Mrs. Taylor sure seems to use a lot of ice whenever he's away.
   And Mr. Baker, can you tell us why your secretary had to leave this town?
   And shouldn't widow Jones be told to keep her window shades all pulled completely down?

5. Well, Mr. Harper couldn't be here 'cause he stayed too long at Kelly's bar again.
   And if you smell Shirley Thompson's breath, you'll find she's had a little nip of gin.
   Then you have the nerve to tell me you think that as a mother I'm not fit.
   Well, this is just a little Peyton Place and you're all Harper Valley hypocrites.
   No, I wouldn't put you on, because it really did, it happened just this way,
   The day my mama socked it to the Harper Valley P-T.A.

Heartbreak Hotel

Words and Music by Mae Boren Axton, Tommy Durden and Elvis Presley

lone - ly I could die._____

Last time fade on these two bars

2. Al-
3. _____

2. though it's al - ways crowd - ed, still can find__ some room,
3. Bell-hop's tears keep flow - ing, desk clerk's dressed in black,

Where those brok - en - heart -ed lov - ers ___ cry_____ a - way their gloom, Oh!
_____ They been so long on Lone - ly Street they ain't nev - er gonn' come back, Oh!

I get so lone - ly, I get so lone - ly,

After repeat, D. S. %
(to 4th lyric)

Get so lone - ly I could die._____

Hello Walls

Words and Music by Willie Nelson

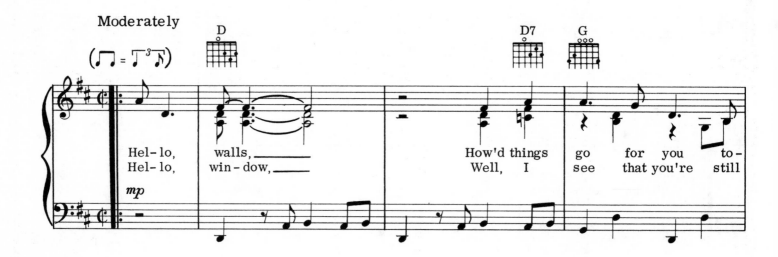

ceil-ing,_____ I'm gon-na stare at you a while. You know I

can't sleep, So won't you bear with me a while? We must

all pull to-geth - er or else I'll lose my mind, 'Cause I've got a

feel-in' she'll be gone a long, long time._____

Help Me Make It Through The Night

Words and Music by Kris Kristofferson

Moderately, in 2 (♩=1 beat)

1. Take the rib-bon from your hair,
2. Come and lay down by my side,

Shake it
Till the

loose and let it fall,
ear-ly morn-in' light,

Lay-in' soft up-on my
All I'm tak-in' is your

skin,
time.

Like the shad-ows on the wall.

Help me make it thru the night. I don't care who's right or wrong, I don't try to under- stand. Let the dev-il take to-mor-row, Lord, to-night I need a friend.

Honey

Words and Music by Bobby Russell

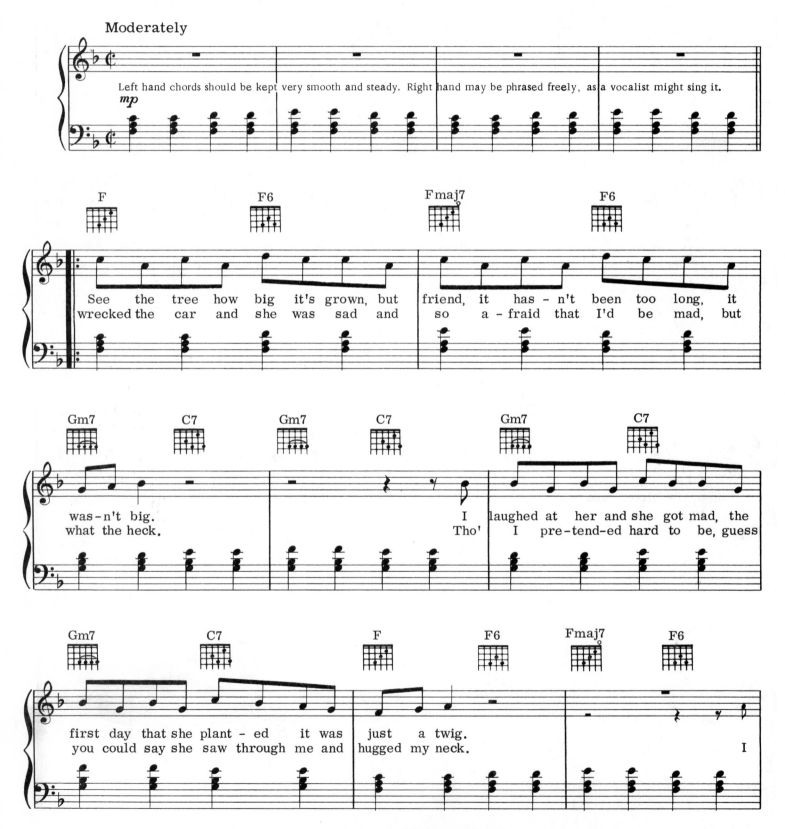

loved her so.
an-gels came.

Now I sur-prised her with a pup-py;
all I have is mem-o-ries of

kept me up all Christ-mas eve two years a-go.
Hon-ey, and I wake up nights and call her name.

And

it would sure em-bar-rass her when I came home from work-ing late 'cause
Now my life's an emp-ty stage where Hon-ey lived and Hon-ey played and

I would know
love grew up.

That she'd been sit-tin' there and cry-in'
A small cloud pass-es o-ver-head and

Honey Be There

Words and Music by Dan Wheetman

Hound Dog

Words and Music by Jerry Leiber and Mike Stoller

I Can't Help But Wonder
(Where I'm Bound)

Words and Music by Tom Paxton

Chorus

And I Can't Help But Won-der where I'm bound, where I'm bound, And I

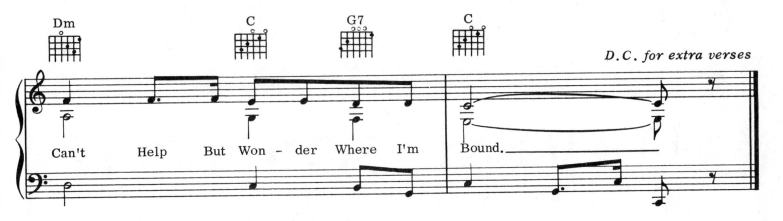

D.C. for extra verses

Can't Help But Won - der Where I'm Bound. _____

Additional Verses

2. I have been around this land
Just a-doin' the best I can
Tryin' to find what I was meant to do.
And the faces that I see
Are as worried as can be
And it looks like they are wonderin' too.
(Chorus)

3. I had a little gal one time
She had lips like sherry wine
And she loved me till my head went plumb insane
But I was too blind to see
She was driftin' away from me
And one day she left on the morning train.
(Chorus)

4. I've got a buddy from home
But he started out to roam
And I hear he's out by Frisco Bay
And sometimes when I've had a few
His voice comes singin' through
And I'm goin' out to see him some old day
(Chorus)

5. If you see me passing by
And you sit and wonder why
And you wish that you were a rambler, too,
Nail your shoes to the kitchen floor
Lace 'em up and bar the door
Thank your stars for the roof that's over you.
(Chorus)

I Fall To Pieces

Words and Music by Hank Cochran and Harlan Howard

never kissed,_____ You want me to for- get, pre-tend we've
else to love,_____ Some- one who'll love me, too, the way you

nev- er met,_____ And I've tried_____ and I've tried, but I
used to do,_____ But each time_____ I go out with__

have- n't yet,_____ You walk by and I fall to
some- one new,_____ You walk by and and I fall to

1.
piec - es._____

2.
piec - es.
rall.

Hitch-Hiker

Words and Music by Dick Reicheg and Eric Weissberg

only things I own, and though I've tried to set-tle

down _____ in man-y a cit-y and town, _____ the

on — ly time I'm hap - py is when I'm ram - blin'

'round. _____   You might

'round. _____

I Never Will Marry

Moderately

New Words and New Music by Fred Hellerman

on — ly he's man gone I ev — er loved Has
gone, many a change like the morn — ing dew, And
young man's heart, But

gone on the morn — ing — train.
left — me all a — lone. I nev — er will
nev — er a change in — mine.

Chorus

mar — ry, — I'll — be no man's wife, — I ex-

pect to live — sin — gle — All the days of my

Last time to Coda

life.

2. Well, the

life.

D. S. al Coda 𝄋

Coda

life.

slower - - - - - - - - - -

I Walk The Line

Words and Music by Johnny Cash

126

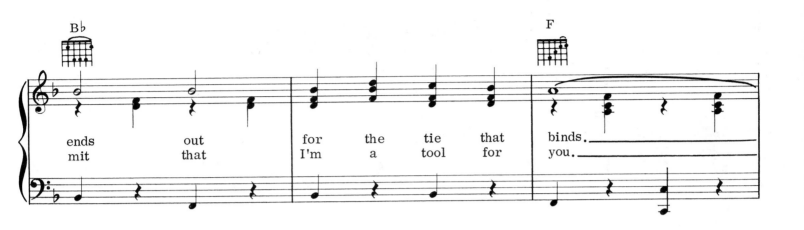

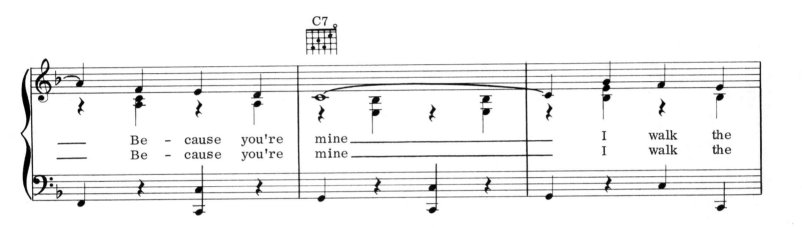

3. As sure as night is dark and day is light,
   I keep you on my mind both day and night.
   And happiness I've known proves that it's right.
   Because you're mine I walk the line.

4. You've got a way to keep me on your side.
   You give me cause for love that I can't hide.
   For you I know I'd even try to turn the tide.
   Because you're mine I walk the line.

5. I keep a close watch on this heart of mine.
   I keep my eyes wide open all the time.
   I keep the ends out for the tie that binds.
   Because you're mine I walk the line.

I Was There

Words and Music by Don Reid

D. S. al Coda

Coda

131

I Will Always Love You

Words and Music by Dolly Parton

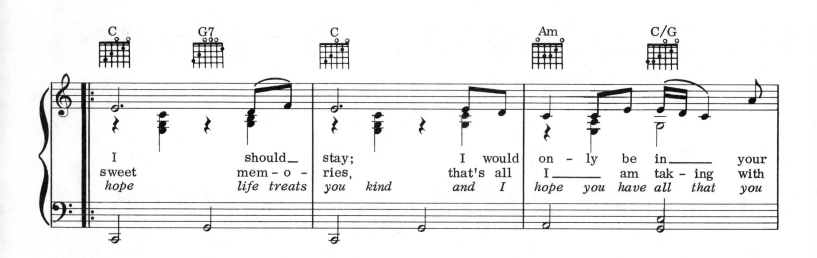

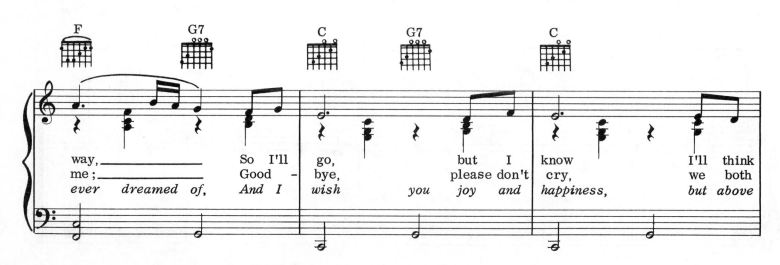

of you each step_____ of the way,_____ And
know that I'm not_____ what you need,_____ But
all of this, I_____ wish you love._____ (Sung): And

I_____ will al - ways_____ love_____

you;_____ I_____ will al - ways_____ love_____

1. 2.

you.   Bit - ter
(Recite): I

3.

you.

I'll Go To My Grave Loving You

Words and Music by Don Reid

Moderately, in 2 (♩ = 1 beat)

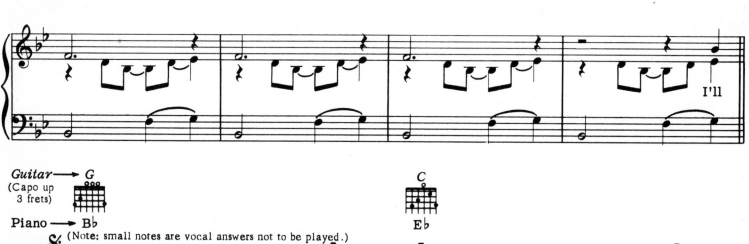

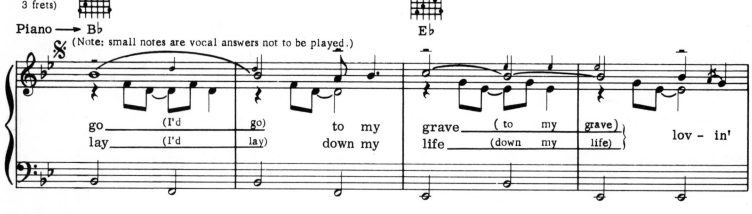

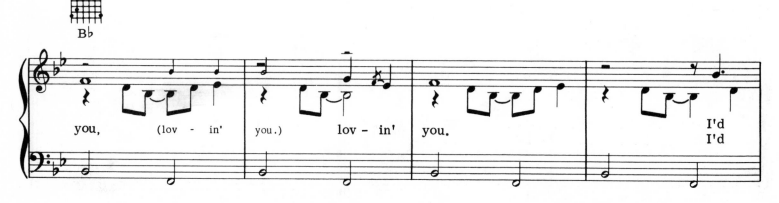

134

136

what a man ____ real-ly is. ____

D. S. al Coda 𝄋

I'd

Coda

B♭

you. ____ (Instrumental)

137

I'm Just A Country Boy

Words and Music by Fred Hellerman and Marshall Barer

Chorus

139

I'm Leaving It (All) Up To You

Words and Music by Don Harris and Dewey Terry, Jr.

Slow Rock tempo

141

It Wasn't God
Who Made Honky Tonk Angels

Words and Music by J. D. Miller

Moderately

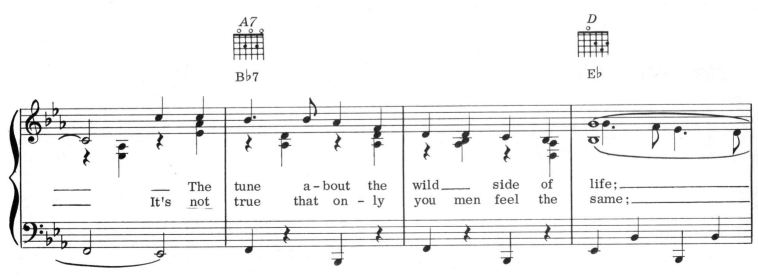

As I 'lis - ten to the words_____ you are say - ing,_____
From the start most ev - 'ry heart that's ev - er bro - ken,_____

It brings mem - 'ries when I was a trust - ing wife._____
Was be - cause there al - ways was a man to blame._____

Chorus

It was - n't God who made honk - y tonk an - gels,_____ As you said in the

Jimmy Brown The Newsboy

Words and Music by A. P. Carter

C7

clothes are torn___ and thin,_____ I
heard my moth - er say,_____
look at me___ and frown,_____ I

And I wan-der a-bout___ from
I am___ help - ing
sell the___ morn - ing

F

Chorus

place to place_____ My dai - ly bread to win.___
Moth-er, sir,___ As I jour - ney on my way.___
pa-pers, sir,_____ My name is Jim-mie Brown.___

I

F

C7

sell the morn-ing pa-pers, sir,___ My name is Jim - mie Brown, Most

F

D. C.
(To Intro)
(Last time to Fine)

ev - 'ry - bod-y knows I am___ The news-boy of the town.

Jolene

Words and Music by Dolly Parton

149

151

King Of The Road

Moderately, with a bounce

Words and Music by Roger Miller

Little Green Apples

Rather slowly

Words and Music by Bobby Russell

154

sum-mer time.__
win-ter comes.__

There's no such thing as Doc-tor Suess,
There's no such thing as make be-lieve,

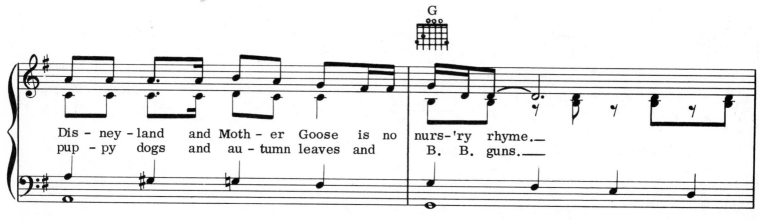

Dis-ney-land and Moth-er Goose is no nurs-'ry rhyme.__
pup-py dogs and au-tumn leaves and B. B. guns.__

God did-n't make lit-tle green ap-ples and it don't rain in In-dian-ap-'lis in the

sum-mer-time,__

And when my-self is feel-in' low I

The Long Black Veil

Words and Music by Marijohn Wilkin and Danny Dill

Love Me Tender

Words and Music by Elvis Presley and Vera Matson

Moderately slow

Verse

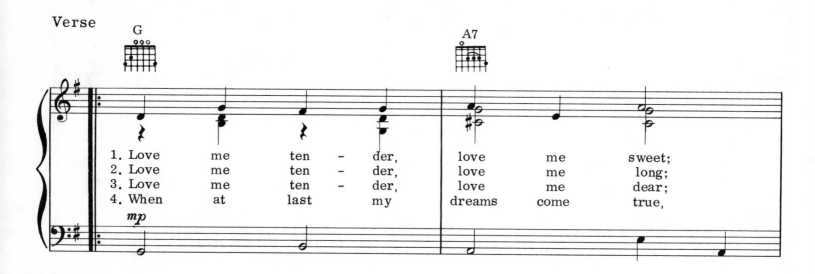

1. Love me ten - der, love me sweet;
2. Love me ten - der, love me long;
3. Love me ten - der, love me dear;
4. When at last my dreams come true,

Nev - er let me go.   You have made my
Take me to your heart.   For it's there that
Tell me you are mine.   I'll be yours through
Dar - ling, this I know: Hap - pi - ness will

Lou'siana Young

Words and Music by Ron Shaw

Love Of The Common People

Words and Music by John Hurley and Ronnie Wilkins

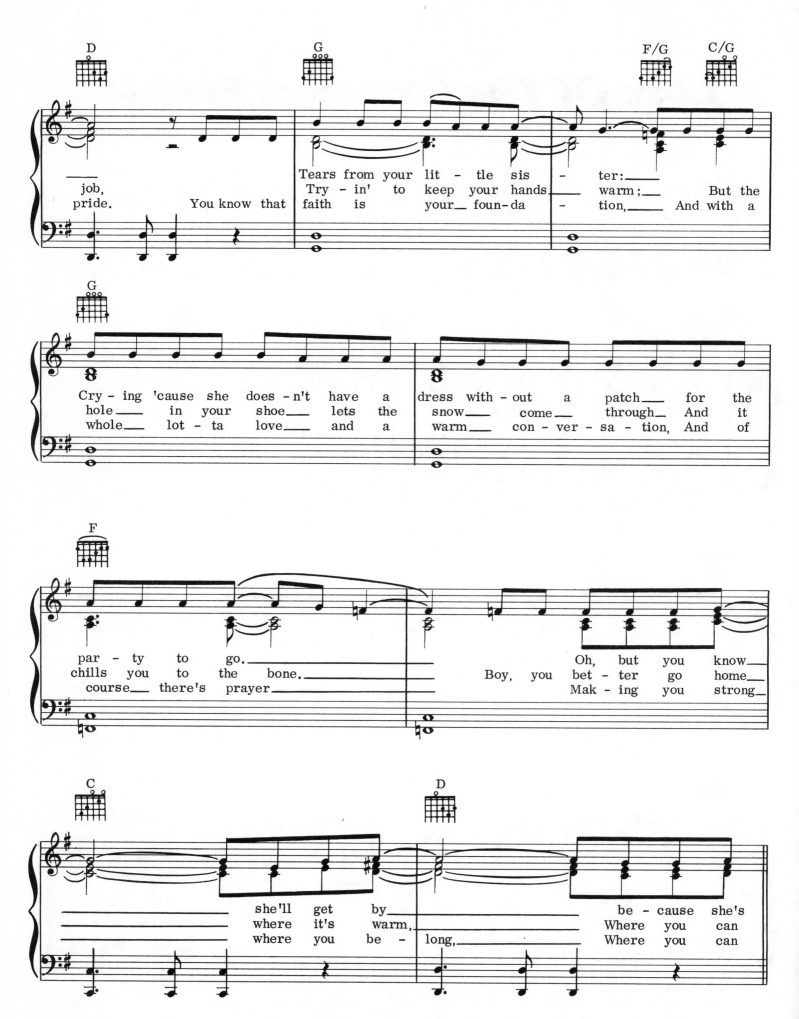

Love Or Something Like It

Words and Music by Kenny Rogers and Steve Glassmeyer

Moderately, with a reggae touch

Show me a bar____ with__ a good look-ing wom - an,_____
That's when I asked__ her_____ "My place or your____ place?____

then just get out__ of my way.___ Turn on the juke - box,__ I'll
I hope I'm not__ out of line."___ I asked the wrong_ thing__ to

show you a song__ you should play.___
just the right wom - an this time.___

Soon - er or lat - er,_____ a | few shots of bour - bon,_____
She knew a ho - tel,_____ she | e - ven had a name we could

I'll think of some - thing to say.____ | Wo,____ I can | take her or leave__ her____
sign._____ | Wo,____ the | cheap-er the grapes_ are__ the

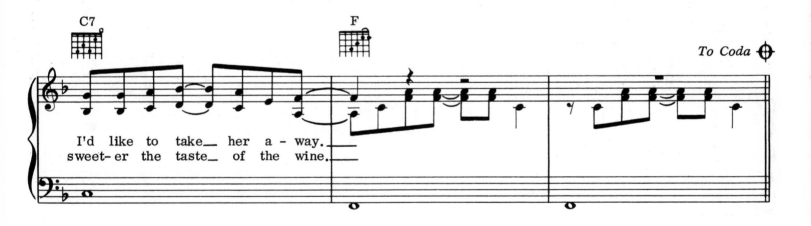

To Coda ⊕

I'd like to take__ her a - way.____ |
sweet-er the taste_ of the wine.____ |

Li-quor and mu - sic,__ A | good com-bi - na - tion__ | if you've got love_ on the brain.

Lucille

Words and Music by R. Bowling and H. Bynum

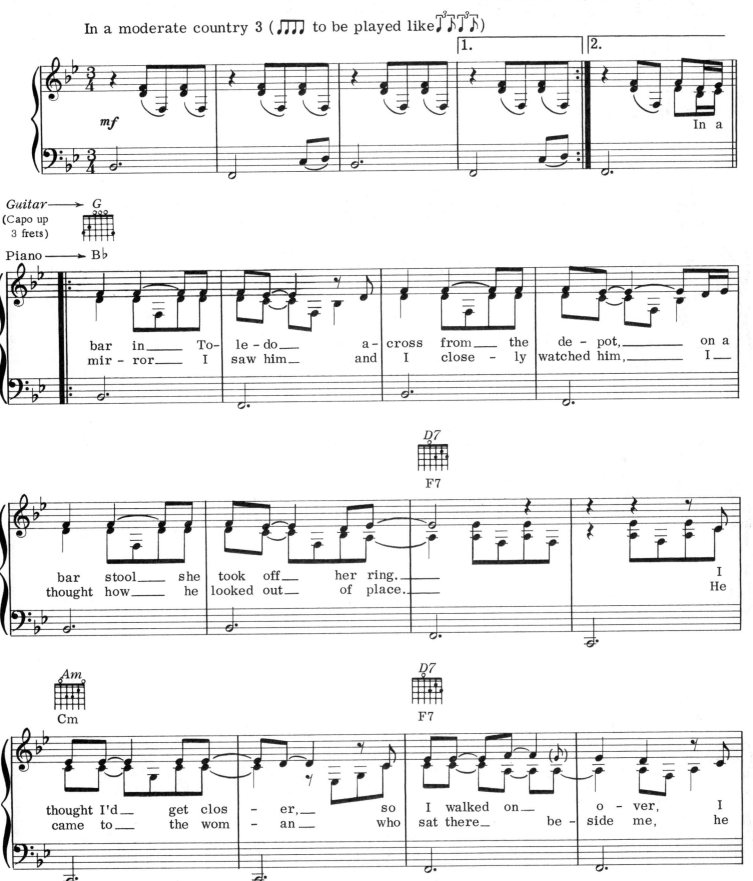

176

bad times,___ lived through_ some sad times,___ but this time_____ your

hurt - in' won't heal,   You picked a fine time_____ to

leave me, Lu - cille.

Af - ter_____ he left us_____ I or - dered_ more_ whis - key,_____ I

178

179

must-'ve thought I'd lost my mind; I could-n't hold___ her___ 'cause the words that he told___ her___ kept com-ing___ back time af-ter time: You picked a fine time to leave___ me, Lu-cille, With

four hun - gry chil - dren and a crop in the field.

I've had___ some bad times,___ lived through___ some

sad times,___ but this time___ your hurt - in' won't heal,

You picked a fine time___ to leave me, Lu - cille.

Repeat and fade

You picked a

Make The World Go Away

Words and Music by Hank Cochran

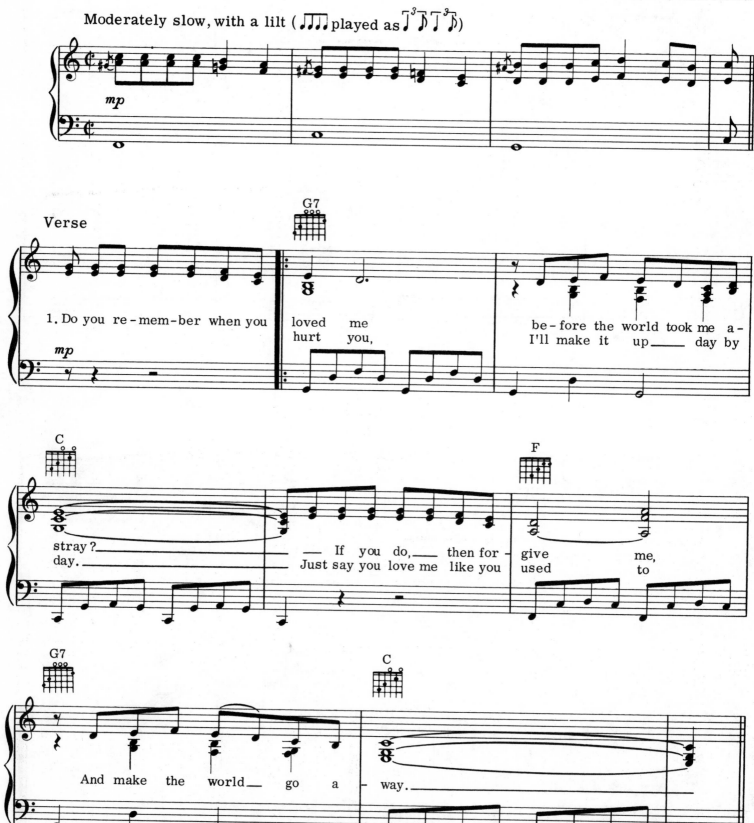

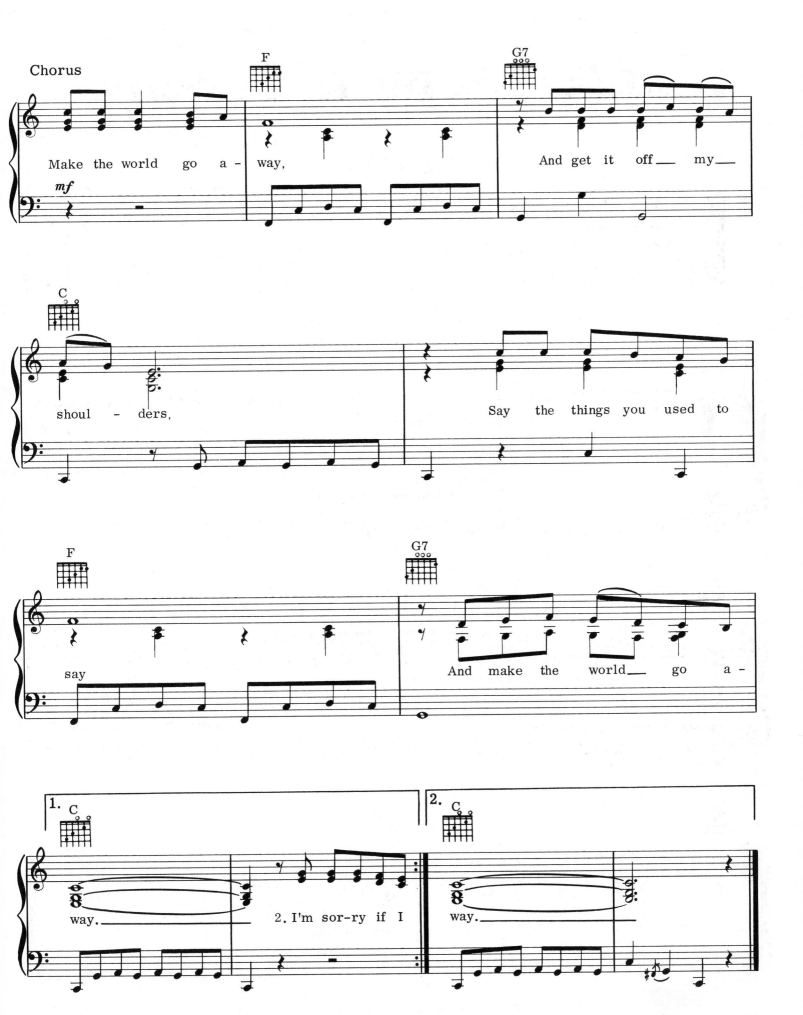

Mammas Don't Let Your Babies Grow Up To Be Cowboys

Words and Music by Ed Bruce and Patsy Bruce

Lone star belt buck-les___ and old fad - ed
Them that don't know him___ won't like him and

Le - vis and each night be - gins___ a new day.___
them that do some-times won't know how___ to take him,

If you
He ain't

don't un - der - stand him and he don't die___ young,
wrong, he's just dif - f'rent but his pride___ won't___ let him do

he'll prob - 'ly
things to make

just ride___ a - way.
you think___ he's right.

Chorus

Mam-mas, don't let your ba - bies grow up to be cow - boys, Don't let them__ pick gui - tars__ and drive them old__ trucks, Let them__ be doc - tors and law - yers and such.

Mam - mas,___ don't let your ba - bies grow up to be

cow - boys, 'cause they'll

nev - er___ stay home and they're al - ways a - lone___ e - ven___ with

After repeat
D. S. and fade 𝄋

some - one they love.___

(Lying Here With)
Linda On My Mind

Moderately slow

Words and Music by Conway Twitty

To next strain

side_ her with Lin-da__ on ____ my mind.   Yes, I

Fine

mind._____   *rit.*

know   that I once   loved her   and I   place__ no one   a-
loved   you for a   long time,   but you're   mar - ried to   a

bove__ her,__   And I   nev - er   thought__ I'd   ev - er   set   her
friend__ of__ mine,__   And   I try   hard__ to   nev - er   let   it

free,___ But it just was-n't in___ my plans___ the
show,___ But my___ love for you is strong-er,___ I can't

1.
way___ Lin-da squeezed___my hand the first time that I held___ her close

as she danced___with me.___ She said, "I've

2.
hide___ it an-y___ long-er.___ And

so___ I thought I'd bet-ter___ let you know."___

D. C. al Fine

190

Me And Bobby McGee

Words and Music by Kris Kristofferson and Fred Foster

poon out of___ my | dirt-y red ban-|dan-na And was |blow-in' sad_ while |Bob-by sang the
lin-as, Lord,_ I | let her slip a - |way Look-in' for_ the |home I hope she'll

blues;_____ |___ With them |wind-shield wip-ers |slap-pin' time and |Bob-by clap-pin'
find;_____ |___ And I'd trade |all of my to - |mor-rows for a |sin-gle yes-ter-

hands We fin-'ly |sang up ev-'ry |song that driv-er__ |knew.}
day, Hold-in' Bob-|by's bod-y next to__ |mine.}

Free-dom's just an-|oth-er__ word for |noth-in'_ left to lose,__

mf

192

Mockin' Bird Hill

Words and Music by Vaughn Horton

Chorus

Tra - la - la, twit-tle-dee - dee - dee, it gives me a thrill To

wake up in the morn-in' to the mock-in' bird's trill; Tra-la- la, twit-tle-dee-

dee - dee, there's peace and good- will; You're wel - come as the flow - ers on

1. 2.

Mock - in' Bird Hill. 2. Got a
3. When it's

3.

Mock - in' Bird Hill.

slower

My Elusive Dreams

Words and Music by Curly Putman and Billy Sherrill

didn't find it there so we moved on.____
didn't find it there so we moved on.____
cling to and____ still you won't let me go on a-lone.

Chorus

I know you're tired of fol-low-ing my e-lu-sive

dreams and schemes,____ For they're on-ly fleet-ing things,

my e-lu-sive dreams.____ 2. You dreams.
3. ____

197

My Ramblin' Boy

Words and Music by Tom Paxton

Moderately

1. He was a man _____ and a friend al- ways, _____ He stuck with
(2. In Tul-sa) town _____ we__ chanced to stray, _____ We thought we'd
(3. __ Late one) night _____ in a jun-gle camp, _____ The weath-er
(4. He left me) there _____ to__ ram-ble on, _____ My ram-blin'

me _____ in the hard old days, _____ He nev-er cared _____ if I had no
try _____ to__ work one day. _____ The boss said he _____ had__ room for
it _____ was__ cold and damp. _____ He got the chills _____ and he got 'em
pal _____ is__ dead and gone. _____ If when we die _____ we__ go some-

dough,_____ We ram-bled
one;_____ Says my old
bad,_____ They took the
where,_____ I'll bet you a

round_____ in the rain and
pal,_____ "We'd_ rath - er
on - ly_ friend I
dollar_____ he's_ ram-blin'

snow._____
bum!"_____
had._____
there._____ } And here's to

you,_____ my ram-blin' boy,_____ May all your ram - blin' bring you

joy._____ And here's to you,_____ my ram-blin' boy,_____ May all your

ram - blin' bring you

1. 2. 3.

joy._____ 2. In Tul-sa
3. _ Late one
4. He left me

4.

joy._____

Okie From Muskogee

Words and Music by Merle Haggard and Roy Edward Burris

right and be-ing free._____
San Fran-cis-co do._____
spect the col-lege dean._____

Chorus

And I'm proud to be an O-kie from Mus-ko-gee;

A place where ev-en squares can have a ball._____

We still wave Ol' Glor-y down at the Court House,

White light-ning's still the big-gest thrill of all._____

1. 2.

3.

2._____
3.Leath-er

Ode To Billy Joe

Words and Music by Bobbie Gentry

off   the   Tal - la - hat-chee   Bridge."

2. Papa said to Mama, as he passed around the black-eyed peas,
   "Well, Billy Joe never had a lick o' sense, pass the biscuits please,
   There's five more acres in the lower forty I've got to plow."
   And Mama said it was a shame about Billy Joe anyhow.
   Seems like nothin' ever comes to no good up on Choctaw Ridge,
   And now Billy Joe **McAllister's** jumped off the Tallahatchee Bridge.

3. Brother said he recollected when he and Tom and Billy Joe,
   Put a frog down my back at the Carroll County picture show,
   And wasn't I talkin' to him after church last Sunday night,
   I'll have another piece of apple pie, you know, it don't seem right.
   I saw him at the sawmill yesterday on Choctaw Ridge,
   And now you tell me Billy Joe's jumped off the Tallahatchee Bridge.

4. Mama said to me, "Child, what's happened to your appetite?
   I been cookin' all mornin' and you haven't touched a single bite,
   That nice young preacher Brother Taylor dropped by today,
   Said he'd be pleased to have dinner on Sunday, Oh, by the way,
   He said he saw a girl that looked a lot like you up on Choctaw Ridge,
   And she an' Billy Joe was throwin' somethin' off the Tallahatchee Bridge."

5. A year has come and gone since we heard the news 'bout Billy Joe,
   Brother married Becky Thompson, they bought a store in Tupelo,
   There was a virus goin' 'round, Papa caught it and died last spring,
   And now Mama doesn't seem to want to do much of anything.
   And me I spend a lot of time pickin' flowers up on Choctaw Ridge,
   And drop them into the muddy water off the Tallahatchee Bridge.

Oklahoma Hills

Words and Music by Woody Guthrie and Jack Guthrie

Paper Roses

Words and Music by Janice Torre and Fred Spielman

Moderately slow, with expression

The Pill

Words and Music by Lorene Allen, Don McHan and T.D. Bayless

Moderately fast

mf

G

You
(I'm)

wined ____ me and
All these years I've
tired of all your

dined ____ me ____ ____
stayed at home ____ while
crow-in' 'bout ____ how

when I was your
you had all your
you and your hens

G

girl, ____ ____ —
fun, ____ ____ And
play, ____ While

Prom-ised if I'd
ev-'ry year that's
hold-in' a cou-ple

be your wife ____
gone ____ by an-
in my arms an-

you'd show me the
oth-er ba-by's
oth-er's on the

D7   **G**   **C**

world,
come,
way.

But
There's
This

all I've seen of
gon-na be some
chick-en's done tore

this old world ____ is a
chang-es made ____ right ____
up her nest ____ and I'm

bed and a doc-tor
here on ____ Nurs-'ry
read-y to make a

bill, _____ I'm __ tear - in' down your brood - er house 'cause
Hill, _____ You've __ set this chick - en your last time, 'cause
deal, _____ And you can't af - ford to turn it down 'cause you

now I've got the pill. _____ (to repeat)
now I've got the pill. _____ (to 2nd ending and Chorus 1)
know I've got the pill. _____ (to 3rd ending and Chorus 2)

1.

2. 3.

Chorus 1. This
Chorus 2. This

old ma - ter - ni - ty dress I've got __ is go - in' in the
in - cu - bat - or is o - ver used __ be - cause you kept it

gar - bage, _____ The clothes I'm wear - in' from now on __ won't
filled, _____ The feel - ing good comes eas - y now __ __

take up so much yard - age! _____ ___ Min - i skirts and
since I've got the pill! _____ It's get-tin' dark, it's

hot pants with a few lit - tle fan - cy frills,_____ Yeah, I'm
roost - ing time, to - night's too good to be real,_____ And ___

mak - in' up for all those years, ___ since I've got the pill._
Dad - dy, don't you wor - ry none, 'cause Ma - ma's got the pill._

To Coda ⊕

D.S. al Coda 𝄋

_____ (to Coda) I'm

Coda ⊕

Please Daddy
(Don't Get Drunk This Christmas)

Words and Music by Bill Danoff and Taffy Nivert

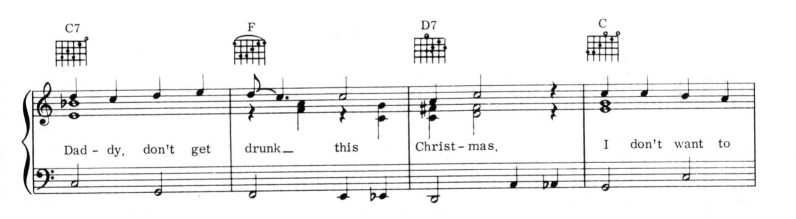

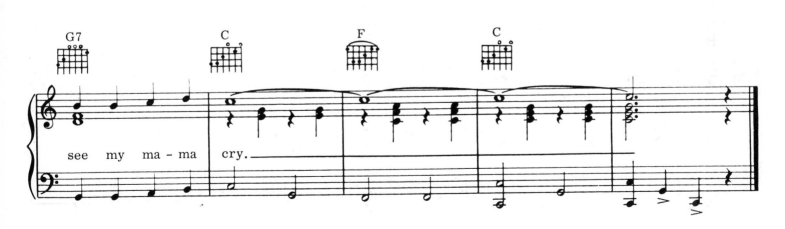

River Of Love

Words and Music by John Martin Sommers

be - come__ some - one__ else - 's bride.__
dar - lin' won't you come back__ home_ a - gain.__ Oh the
nev - er ev - er see your__ smile_ a - gain.__

riv - er__ of love__ it has__ gone__ mud - dy and the

flow - ers they are dy - ing on the shore.__ And the

blue skies have all__ turned to dark - ness and the

night - in - gale___ will sing no___ more.

more.   To-mor-   more   And the

blue skies   have all___ turned to dark-ness___   and the

night - in - gale___ will sing no___   more.___

218

Ruby,
Don't Take Your Love To Town

Words and Music by Mel Tillis

The shad-ow on the wall___ tells me the sun is go-in' down.___
yes, it's true___ that___ I'm not the man I used to be.___

Oh, Ru -
Oh, Ru -

by,___
by,___

don't
I still

take your love to town.___
need some com - pa - ny.___

It
It's

221

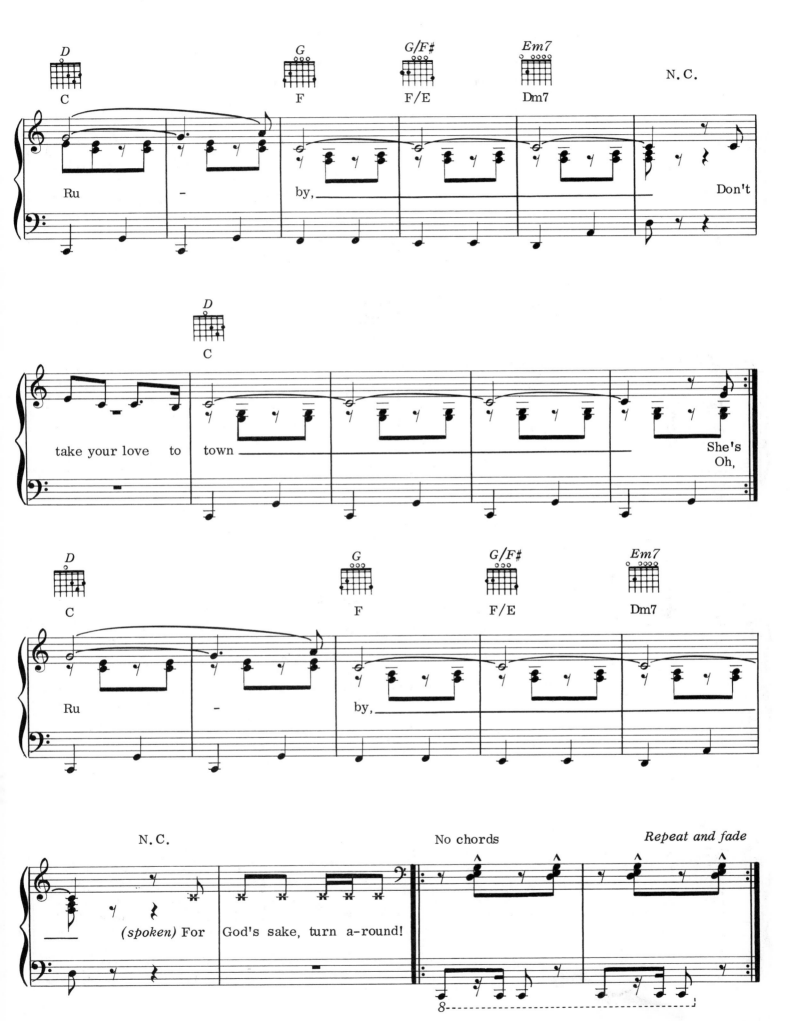

She's Got You

Words and Music by Hank Cochran

Susan When She Tried

Words and Music by Don Reid

Sweet Music Man

Words and Music by Kenny Rogers

no-bod-y else could make__ me feel__ that things are right__ when I know__ they're wrong.__

No-bod-y sings a love__ song__ quite like you.

Verse 2

Sing your song, sweet mu-sic man,__ You

trav-el the world__ with a six piece band__ that does__ for you what you

ask 'em to. And you try to stay young but the songs you've sung to

so many people they've all begun to come back on you.

So sing your song, sad music man,

You're makin' your livin' doin' one-night stands that

prove to you they don't need you. You're still a

Take Me Home, Country Roads

Words and Music by Bill Danoff, Taffy Nivert and John Denver

Ten More Nights
In This Old Barroom

Words and Music by Pat and Victoria Garvey

all   is   no sound at   all. ____

Here I sit

watch-ing you   re- shape the pil-low, ___ the cov-er - let's   stained,   just the

dirt   and   the creas - es   re - main. ____

D. S. al Coda

Coda

down.
Slower

Teddy Bear

Words and Music by Dale Royal, Billy Joe Burnette, Red Sovine and Tommy Hill

Moderately bright

242

(RECITATION:) I was on the outskirts of a little southern town; trying to reach
my destination before the sun went down... The CB was blaring away on
channel 19... when there came a little boy's voice on the radio line...
He said: "Breaker 19!... Is anyone there? Come on back, truckers... and
talk to Teddy Bear!"... I keyed the mike and said: "You got it, Teddy Bear!"
And a little boy's voice came back on the air... "'Preciate the break,...
Who we got on that end?"...
I told him my handle and he began:...

"I'm not supposed to bother you fellows out there... Mom says you're busy and
for me to stay off the air... But you see, I get lonely and it helps to talk...
'cause that's all I can do... I'm crippled,... I can't walk!!!"

I came back and told him to fire up that mike... and I'd talk to him as long
as he liked... "This was my dad's radio" the little boy said... "But I
guess it's mine and mom's now, 'cause my dad's dead!"

"He had a wreck about a month ago... He was trying to get home in a blinding
snow... Mom has to work now, to make ends meet... and I'm not much help with
my two crippled feet!"

"She says not to worry... that we'll make it alright... But I hear her crying
sometimes late at night... There's just one thing I want more than anything to
see... Aw, I know you guys are too busy to bother with me!"

"But my dad used to take me for rides when he was home... but that's all over
now, since my daddy's gone..." ... Not one breaker came on the old CB
as the little crippled boy talked with me... I tried to swallow a lump that
wouldn't stay down... as I thought about my boy back in Greenville Town.

"Dad was going to take mom and me with him later on this year... I remember
him saying: 'Someday this old truck will be yours, Teddy Bear!'... But I know
now I will never get to ride an 18 wheeler again... but this old bas will keep
me in touch with all my trucker friends!"

"Teddy Bear's gonna back on out now and leave you alone 'cause it's about time
for Mom to come home... Give me a shout when you're passing through... and
I'll surely be happy to come back to you!"

I came back and said: "Before you go, 10-10... what's your home 20, little
CB friend?"... He gave me his address and I didn't once hesitate... this
hot load of freight would just have to wait!

I turned that truck around on a dime and headed for Jackson Street, 229...
I round the corner and got one heck of a shock... 18 wheelers were lined up
for three city blocks!

Every driver for miles around had caught Teddy Bear's call... and that little
crippled boy was having a ball... For as fast as one driver would carry him
in, another would carry him to his truck and take off again.

Well, you better believe I took my turn riding Teddy Bear... and then carried
him back in and put him down on his chair... And if I never live to see happiness
again... I saw it that day in the face of that little man.

We took up a collection for him before his mama got home... Each driver said
goodbye and then they were gone... He shook my hand with his mile-long grin
and said: "So long, trucker... I'll catch you again!"

I hit the Interstate with tears in my eyes... I turned on the radio and got
another surprise... "Breaker 19!" Came the voice on the air... "Just one word
of thanks from Mama Teddy Bear!"

"We wish each and every one a special prayer for you... you made a little crippled
boy's dream come true... I'll sign off now, before I start to cry...
May God ride with you... 10-4... and goodbye!"

Thank God I'm A Country Boy

Moderately

Words and Music by John Martin Sommers

Well, life on a farm is kind-a laid back, ain't
work's all ___ done and the sun's ___ settin' low I
wouldn't trade my life for dia-monds or jewels, I
fid-dle was my daddy's till the day he died, and he

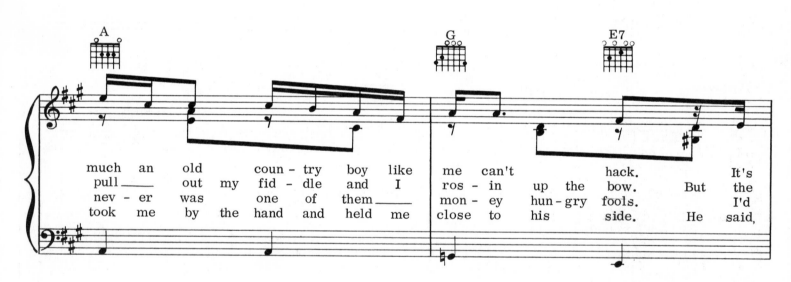

much an old coun-try boy like me can't hack. It's
pull ___ out my fid-dle and I ros-in up the bow. But the
nev-er was one of them ___ mon-ey hun-gry fools. I'd
took me by the hand and held me close to his side. He said,

ear-ly to rise, ear-ly in the sack: Thank
kids ___ are a-sleep so I keep it kind-a low: Thank
rath-er have my fid-dle and my farm-in' ___ tools: Thank
"Live a good life and play my fid-dle with ___ pride, And thank

245

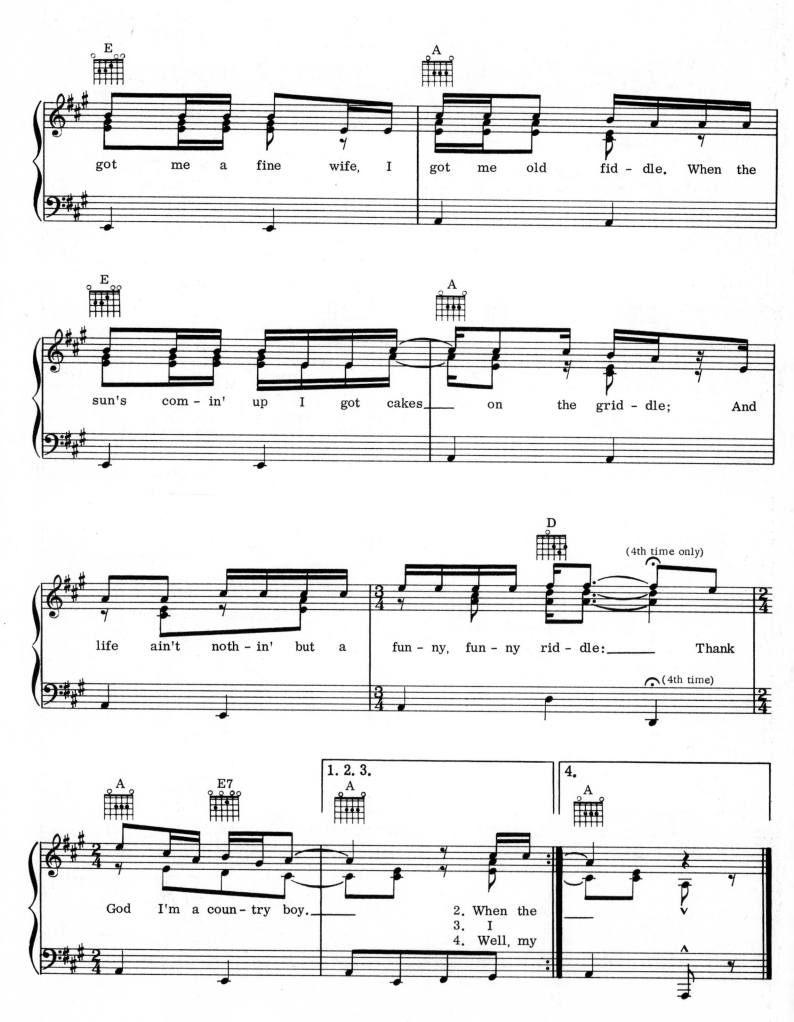

got me a fine wife, I got me old fid-dle. When the

sun's com-in' up I got cakes___ on the grid-dle; And

life ain't noth-in' but a fun-ny, fun-ny rid-dle:___ Thank

(4th time only)

(4th time)

God I'm a coun-try boy.___

1. 2. 3.
2. When the
3. I
4. Well, my

4.

Torn Between Two Lovers

Words and Music by Peter Yarrow and Phillip Jarrell

hold you close_ and say these words as | gent-ly as I | can.

There's been an-oth-er man that I've | need - ed____ and I've loved,_
You must-n't think you failed me just be- | cause there's some-one___ else,_You were the

But that does-n't mean I love you | less.
first real___ love___ I ev - er had. And he

knows he can't pos - sess me, and he | knows he nev - er will, There's just this
And all the things I ev -er said,_____ I | swear they still are true_____ For
_____ I could-n't real-ly blame you if you | turned and walked a-way,____ But with

248

Today I Started Loving You Again

Words and Music by Merle Haggard and Bonnie Owens

Moderately slow

Well, to-day I start-ed lov-ing you again. Now I'm right back where I've real-ly al-ways been. I got o-ver you just

251

With on - ly these few mil-lion tears I've cried.

I should have known___ the worst___ was yet___ to

come And that cry - in' time___ for

me had just be - gun.___ Well, to-

D.S. al Coda

252

Waterloo

Words and Music by John D. Loudermilk and Marijohn Wilkin

Whatever Happened To Randolph Scott

Words and Music by Don Reid and Harold Reid

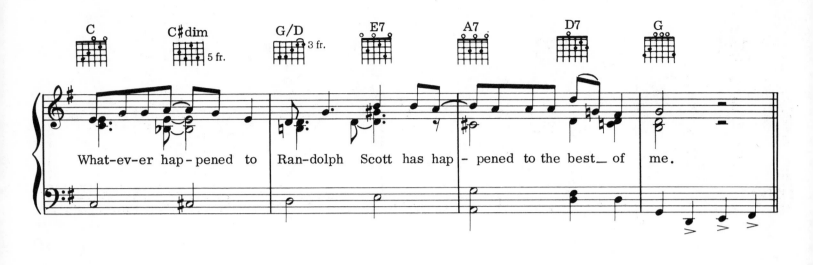

What-ev-er hap-pened to Ran-dolph Scott has hap-pened to the best_ of me.

N.C.

Verse 2

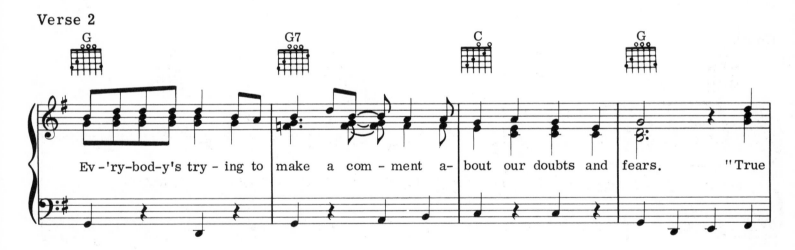

Ev-'ry-bod-y's try-ing to make a com-ment a-bout our doubts and fears. "True

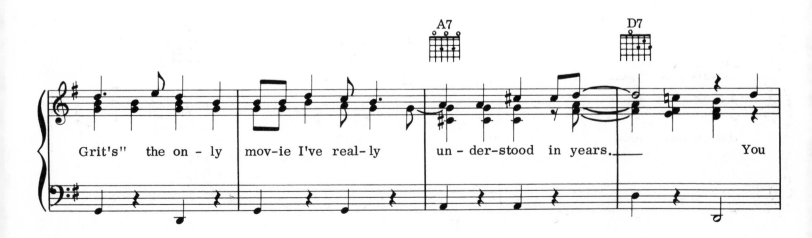

Grit's" the on-ly mov-ie I've real-ly un-der-stood in years.___ You

got - ta take_ your an-a-lyst a-long to see if it's fit to see.

What-ev-er hap-pened to Ran-dolph Scott has hap-pened to the in - dus - try.

Chorus

What-ev-er hap-pened to John-ny Mack Brown and_ Al-lan Rock-y Lane?

What-ev-er hap-pened to Lash La-rue,_ I'd_ love to see them a - gain.

Wildwood Flower

Adapted and Arranged by Dan Fox

1. I will
(2. Oh, he)
(3. I will)

min - gle my tress - es of ra - ven black
taught me to love him and my called me his
dance, I will sing him and my heart will be

hair
flow'r
gay,

With the ros - es so
A bright blos - som to
I will charm ev - 'ry

red and the lil - ies so fair,
cheer him through life's wear - y hour,
heart and drive trou - bles a - way,

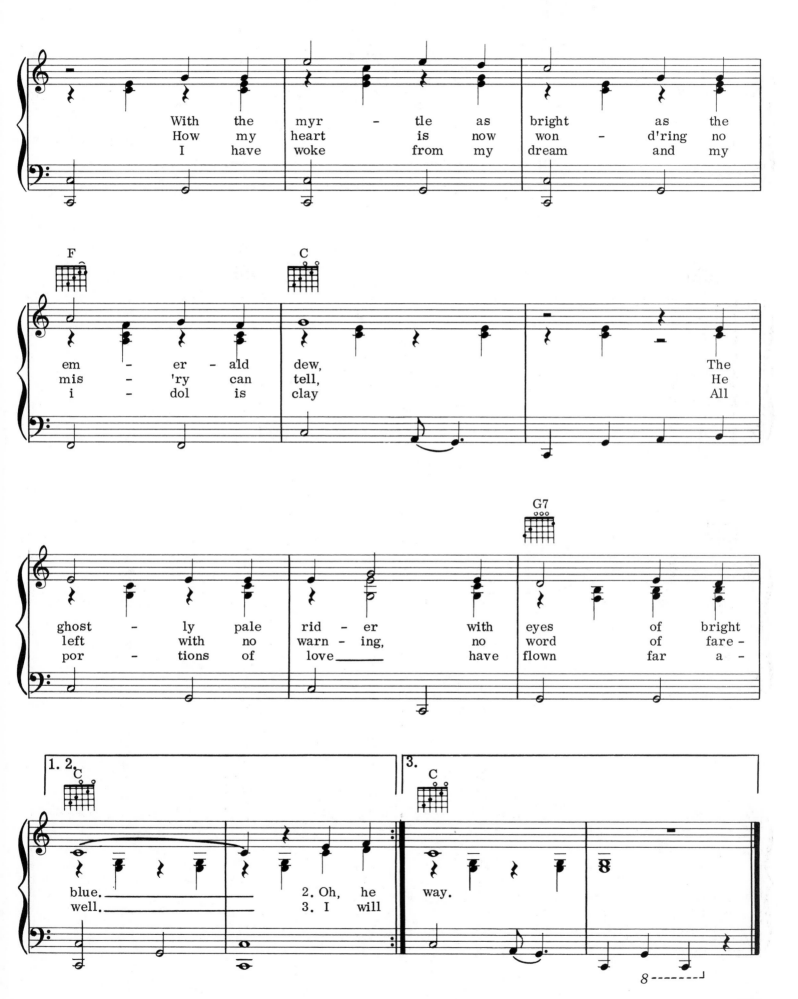

With the myr — tle as bright as the
How my heart is now won — d'ring no my
I have woke from my dream and my

em — er — ald dew, tell, The
mis — 'ry can clay He
i — dol is All

ghost — ly pale rid — er with eyes of bright
left with no warn — ing, no word of fare —
por — tions of love have flown far a —

1. 2.
blue. _____
well. _____
2. Oh, he
3. I will

3.
way.

263

When I Was Young

Words and Music by Jim Friedman and Susan Minsky

Slowly and rather freely

Lyrics:

A cas-tle fell one day,__ my dream was done,__ I said fare-well that day__ when I was young. So you had gone a-way,__ a song half sung,__ I trav-eled on my way__ when I was young. Then lone-ly lost was I__ with burn-ing eye, I chased your shad-ow far__ a-cross the sky.__ I looked a-

Wolverton Mountain

Words and Music by Merle Kilgore and Claude King

Chorus

You've Never Been This Far Before

Words and Music by Conway Twitty

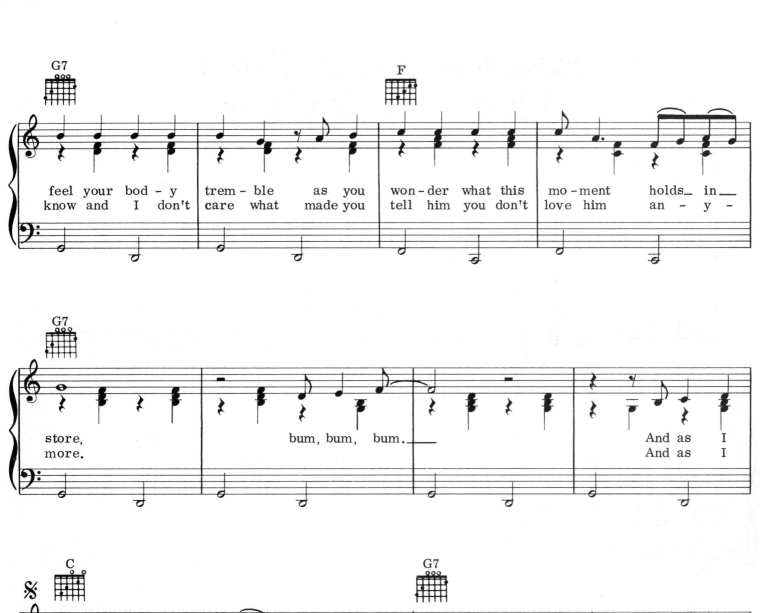

feel your bod - y | trem - ble as you | won - der what this | mo - ment holds_ in_
know and I don't | care what made you | tell him you don't | love him an - y -

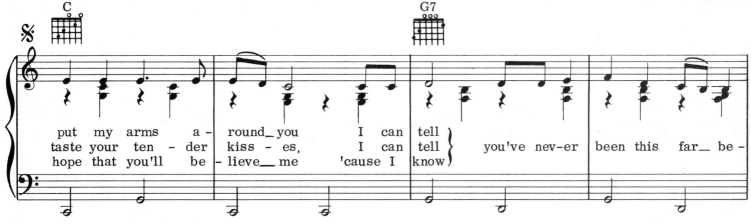

store, | | bum, bum, bum._ | | And as I
more. | | | | And as I

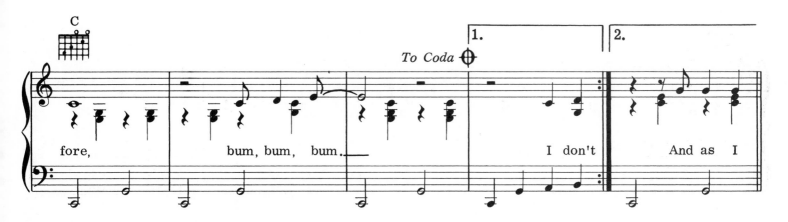

put my arms a - | round_ you I can | tell } you've nev - er been this far_ be -
taste your ten - der | kiss - es, I can | tell }
hope that you'll be - | lieve_ me 'cause I | know }

To Coda

fore, | | bum, bum, bum._ | | I don't | And as I

Yesterday When I Was Young
(Hier Encore)

English lyric by Herbert Kretzmer
Original French text and music by Charles Aznavour

planned   I al-ways built, a - | las,   on weak and shift-ing | sand;   I lived by night and
pride   and ev -'ry flame I | lit   too quick-ly, quick-ly | died;   The friends I made all

To Coda

shunned   the nak-ed light of | day   And on-ly now I | see   how the years ran a-
seemed   some-how to drift a - | way   And on-ly I am | left   on stage to end the

way.   Yes-ter- | day_____ when I was | young,   So man-y drink-ing
   time and youth at last ran | out,   I nev-er stopped to

songs   were wait-ing to be | sung,   So man-y way-ward | plea - sures lay in store for
think   what life was all a - | bout,   And ev -'ry con-ver - | sa - tion I can now re-

274

Index of Composers and Lyricists